FURNESS
RAILWAY

PUBLISHERS' NOTE

This volume of locomotive and stock drawings by Mr. Rush are published as a separate book, and not bound in with the History itself, so that model makers who may only wish to have the drawings, or others whose interest in the subject is mainly historical, will not be put to unnecessary expense.

The Locomotive List is published in both, as it is felt that neither is complete without it.

Locomotive dimensions are shown in the table, and dimensions not shown may be deduced from those which are. In the case of rolling stock, main dimensions are marked on the drawings.

INTRODUCTION

The series of drawings presented here have a two-fold purpose; partly to provide more illustrations for the main history of the Furness Railway than could have been achieved by photographs which, it must be admitted, are very scarce as regards rolling stock in particular but mainly for the interest of model makers, to whom it is hoped they will be of value. All the drawings, with one or two exceptions, have been produced from the official Furness Railway Diagram Books. The original diagrams contained in these books were somewhat crude and lacking in detail, and as far as possible these have been elaborated with the aid of specimen photographs, into drawings which can form a good basis for the modeller to use. It is regretted that owing to the exigencies of publication, a standard scale for all the drawings has not been possible. However, main dimensions are given for all rolling stock, and it should not be too difficult for model makers to obtain from them a workable scale for each item.

Regarding locomotives, dimensions are not given on the drawings, but a complete dimensional table is included, from which most of the other details can be obtained by judicious scaling. No front or rear elevations are given, this is unfortunate, but for some reason unknown, widths over buffer beams, cab sides, or tanks, are very rarely quoted on official diagrams of locomotives, though widths are almost always given in the case of rolling stock. Hence, with the paucity of such data, it was thought better to leave out end elevations of locomotives altogether rather than to make them by guesswork. It is regretted, but it is hoped that the omission will not detract too much from the value of the work as a whole.

Most of the carriage diagrams are included, though one or two have been omitted. For example, Diagram 5 differed only from Diagram 4 in the arrangement of the external mouldings; Diagram 2 was an eight-compartment third similar to Diagram 1, but only 48 feet long. There were three diagrams for passenger brake vans, two of which were 6-wheeled, and the other, which is illustrated, had four wheels. The larger vans were almost identical in layout, one being 30 feet in length, and the other 34 feet. All dimensions are given as over body at the waist line. Most of the carriages had standard under-frames, one each of the 4, 6, and 8-wheeled varieties being shown in detail.

Turning to goods stock, only a representative range of drawings are given. Many of the Furness diagrams differed only in minor details—even down to one inch in width—and therefore it has not been considered necessary to illustrate every diagram. Broadly, the diagrams can be summarised as follows:—

Diagrams	1–17	Open wagons.
"	18–23	Vans.
"	24–35	Ore Wagons.
"	36–37	Coke Wagons.
"	38–39	Loco Coal Wagons.
"	40, 41, 44, 45, 47,	Special Wagons
"	42, 43, 46,	Bolster Wagons
"	48–51	Cattle Wagons.
"	52–54	Goods Brake Vans.

The drawings have been chosen to show a representative selection of each group. Two main types of underframe were used, wood, and steel channel, mostly with either side brake gear, though a number of wagons dating from the 1880's had brakes on one side only. Unless otherwise indicated, wood frames are shown in the drawings. Of the three steel hopper wagons, Diagram 32 had wooden frames, the others being all steel. The bulk of the ore wagons had bottom doors for discharging the cargo into chutes or pits at the various ironworks. No diagram of the huge 45-ton ore wagons has been found; these were probably Diagram 24, which is missing from the author's copy of the Diagram Book; hence it has not been possible to illustrate this particular type. Since the wagons had a very short life of only four or five years, the relevant diagram was probably removed from the book and not re-issued.

No running numbers were given on any of the passenger stock diagrams (except the saloons and mail vans), though the total number built was given. Such numbers as are shown on the drawings are either from photographs, or other brief references. Consequently no complete list can be given, though in the main historical volume both the 1923 and 1933 L.M.S.R. renumberings are given in detail. It has been suggested that the 1923 L.M.S.R. list was made by simply adding 15,000 to the original Furness numbers, but except in the case of the seven saloons, this has been proved to be a false assumption. It may be mentioned in passing that the ordinary passenger stock was numbered from 1 upwards regardless of class, type, or number of wheels, but saloons, passenger brake vans, horse boxes, and the like were each numbered from 1 upwards in separate series.

Likewise, the goods stock diagrams were not fully numbered; though the actual number of each type built was stated, the running numbers were very incomplete. For some obscure reason, it is possible to reconstruct the complete sequence of numbers in the 7000's, (with one or two exceptions), but otherwise, apart from a good proportion of the ore wagons, only odd numbers here and there were mentioned. The total goods stock at 31 December 1921 was returned as 7428, therefore there must have been a number of blanks in the complete list. Further than this it is not possible to go.

Livery: All Furness engines were Indian red (No.29 in Carter's "British Railway Liveries") picked out in black, with a fine vermilion line on either side of the black. Buffer beams were vermilion, lined in black. The letters F.R. appeared on tender sides, or on tanks, in gold, shaded light blue to the left and below Buffer beam numbers or letters were similar. The engine number appeared on a brass plate, with "Furness Railway" round the edge, in raised lettering, and with the background painted black. There were various positions for the number plates; most of the earlier classes had them fixed to the boiler, on the centre line, but later engines had them on the cab side, or on the bunker in the case of tank engines. The Whitehaven, Cleator & Egremont engines however, always had the number plates fixed on the saddle tanks.

The only exception to the Indian red rule was the Class A5 0-4-0 tender engines, which spent their entire career painted black, with vermilion lining.

Passenger stock was dark blue (No.25 in Carter's book), with white upper panels, waist panels were also white, except on the doors, where they were blue. Lettering and numbering, also lining on the external mouldings, were in gold. Underframes were blue, lined in white, while bogie frames and undergear were black. Roofs were light grey. In 1915, as a wartime economy, the white upper panels were changed to blue, and lining became yellow, the white lining on underframes was omitted. The original scheme was never re-instated.

Goods stock was a medium grey, with black ironwork. Lettering was in white; the letters "F.R." were 17½" high and 13½" wide, unless the wagon sides would not allow of this, in which case the lettering was as large as possible. (Bolster wagons, etc.) The number appeared in 6" figures in the left hand lower corner of each side, and was repeated on each end in 3" figures, in a similar position.

Locomotive List

No.	Class	Builders	Date	Withdrawn	Notes
1	A1	BCK	1844	1867	
2	,,	,,	,,	1871	Sold
3	A2	,,	1846	1900	Preserved
4	,,	,,	,,	1898	
5	B1	SB 696	1852	1873	
6	,,	,, 697	,,	1873	
7	A3	F	1854	1899	
8	,,	,,	,,	1899	
9	,,	,,	1855	1901	9A (1899)
10	,,	,,	,,	1900	10A (1899)
11	B2	SB 1016	1857	1873	Sold
12	,,	,, 1017	,,	1898	Sold. 12A (1873)
13	A4	F	1858	1900	13A (1899)
14	,,	,,	,,	1900	14A (1899)
15	,,	,,	1861	1899	
16	,,	,,	,,	1899	16 A
17	A5	SS 1434	1863	1870	Sold
18	,,	,, 1435	,,	1870	Sold
19	,,	,, 1447	,,	1870	Sold
20	,,	,, 1448	,,	1870	Sold
21	B3	,, 1500	1864	1898	21A (1896)
22	,,	,, 1501	,,	1898	Sold. 22A (1896)
23	C1	,, 1543	,,	1904	98 (1898)
24	,,	,, 1544	,,	1904	99 (1898)
25	A5	,, 1585	1865	1873	Sold
26	,,	,, 1586	,,	1873	Sold
27	,,	,, 1663	1866	1918	27A (1914)
28	,,	,, 1664	,,	1918	28A (1914)
29	D1	,, 1697	,,	1925	R/00 T2. 61 (1918) L.M.S. 12001
30	,,	,, 1698	,,	1925	R/99 T2 62 (1918) L.M.S. 12007
31	,,	,, 1764	,,	1925	R/99 T2 48 (1920) L.M.S. 12000
32	,,	,, 1765	,,	1900	32A (1896)
33	,,	,, 1766	,,	1900	33A (1896)
34	B3	,, 1763	,,	1898	34A (1896)
35	,,	,, 1768	,,	1898	Sold. 35A (1896)
36	,,	,, 1767	,,	1898	36A (1896)
37	,,	,, 1762	,,	1898	37A (1896)
38	D1	,, 1760	,,	1915	
39	,,	,, 1761	,,	1915	

No.	Class	Builders	Date			Withdrawn	Notes
40	D1	SS 1784	1866			1925	R/oo T2 80 (1916) L.M.S. 12008
41	,,	,, 1785	,,			1916	
42	D2	H 1269	1864 Ex WFJ	19		1904	R/86
43	,,	,, 1245	,, ,, ,,	18		1873	Sold
44	F1	,, 997	1857 ,, ,,	3		1882	
45	,,	,, 998	,, ,, ,,	13		1882	
46	B4	,, 1148	1860 ,, ,,	10		1876	Sold
47	B5	EBW	1850 ,, ,,	4		1870	Sold
48	,,	,,	,, ,, ,,	5		1870	Sold
49	C2	FJ 29	1862 ,, ,,	15		1882	Sold
50	,,	N 571	1863 ,, ,,	16		1882	Sold
51	G1	SS 1842	1867			1915	
52	,,	,, 1843	,,			1918	84 (1915)
1	E1	,, 2057	1870			1916	1A (1913)
2	,,	,, 2058	,,			1918	2A (1913)
17	D1	,, 2064	1871			1925	R/oo T2 23 (1900) 42 (1910) 66 (1916) L.M.S. 12003
18	,,	,, 2065	,,			1910	24 (1900)
19	,,	,, 2095	,,			1910	
20	,,	,, 2096	,,			1925	R/oo T2 25 (1910) 25A (1913) LMS 12002
53	D1	SS 2097	1871			1916	
54	,,	,, 2098	,,			1925	R/98 T2 78 (1916) LMS 12005
55	,,	,, 2099	,,			1918	
56	,,	,, 2100	,,			1913	
57	E1	,, 2093	,,			1918	
58	,,	,, 2094	,,			1918	
59	,,	,, 2145	,,			1913	
60	,,	,, 2146	,,			1921	R/oo T2 64 (1918)
61	,,	,, 2147	,,			1916	R/oo T2
62	,,	,, 2148	,,			1916	R/99 T2
63	,,	,, 2149	,,			1918	R/oo T2
64	,,	,, 2150	,,			1918	
65	,,	,, 2151	,,			1930	R/18 T4 LMS 12065
66	,,	,, 2152	,,			1916	
67	,,	,, 2153	,,			1914	
43	,,	,, 2154	,,			1925	R/o1 T2 67 (1916) LMS 12004
68	G1	,, 2204	1872			1925	LMS 11549
69	,,	,, 2205	,,			1925	LMS 11550
70	E1	,, 2245	,,			1924	R/91 (2–4–2T) 70A (1920) LMS 10619
71	,,	,, 2246	,,			1923	R/91 (2–4–2T) 71A (1920) LMS 10620
72	,,	,, 2247	,,			1919	R/91 (2–4–2T)
73	,,	,, 2248	,,			1919	R/91 (2–4–2T)
74	,,	,, 2249	,,			1921	R/91 (2–4–2T) 72A (1920)
75	,,	,, 2257	,,			1914	
46	,,	,, 2256	,,			1920	
47	,,	,, 2258	,,			1919	R/91 (2–4–2T)
48	,,	,, 2259	,,			1920	R/91 (2–4–2T)
25	D1	,, 2278	1873			1910	

No.	Class		Works No.	Year	Notes
118	,,	,,	2949	,,	1927 R/11 T3. 73 (1920) LMS 12073
119	,,	,,	2950	,,	1926 R/10 T3. 74 (1920) LMS 12074
44	E1	,,	3086	1882	1925 R/98 44A (1920) LMS 10002
45	,,	,,	3087	,,	1921 R/91 45A (1920)
49	D1	,,	3170	1883	1928 R/16 T4. LMS 12075
50	,,	,,	3171	,,	1928 R/12 T3. LMS 12076
120	,,	,,	3172	,,	1887 Sold
121	,,	,,	3173	,,	1887 Sold
120	K1	,,	3618	1890	1927 LMS 10131
121	,,	,,	3619	,,	1928 LMS 10132
122	,,	,,	3620	,,	1927 LMS 10133
123	,,	,,	3621	,,	1925 LMS 10134
21	K2	,,	4174	1896	1930 32 (1896) 44 (1910) LMS 10137
22	,,	,,	4175	,,	1928 33 (1896) 45 (1910) LMS 10138
34	,,	,,	4176	,,	1927 46 (1920) LMS 10139
35	,,	,,	4177	,,	1928 47 (1920) LMS 10140
36	,,	,,	4178	,,	1929 LMS 10135
37	,,	,,	4179	,,	1931 LMS 10136
112	L1	,,	4364	1898	1927 LMS 11622
113	,,	,,	4365	,,	1928 LMS 11623
114	,,	,,	4366	,,	1928 LMS 11624
7	D3	NW	552	1899	1928 LMS 12468
8	,,	,,	553	,,	1930 LMS 12469 R/25 LY
9	,,	,,	554	,,	1932 LMS 12470
10	,,	,,	555	,,	1930 LMS 12471
11	,,	,,	556	,,	1930 LMS 12472
12	,,	,,	557	,,	1929 LMS 12473
13	,,	SS	4563	,,	1930 LMS 12474
14	,,	,,	4564	,,	1932 LMS 12475
15	,,	,,	4565	,,	1930 LMS 12476
16	,,	,,	4566	,,	1930 LMS 12477
17	,,	,,	4567	,,	1929 LMS 12478
18	,,	,,	4568	,,	1936 LMS 12479 R/25 LY
124	K2	,,	4651	1900	1928 LMS 10141
125	,,	,,	4652	,,	1929 LMS 10142
126	K3	,,	4716	1901	1931 LMS 10143
127	,,	,,	4717	,,	1930 LMS 10144
128	,,	,,	4718	,,	1930 LMS 10145
129	,,	,,	4719	,,	1930 LMS 10146
98	L2	NW	689	1904	1935 LMS 11625
99	,,	,,	690	,,	1930 LMS 11626
100	,,	,,	691	,,	1936 LMS 11627
101	,,	,,	692	,,	1946 LMS 11628
102	,,	,,	693	,,	1930 LMS 11629
103	,,	NBL	16113	,,	1934 LMS 11630 R/27 LY
104	,,	,,	16114	,,	1930 LMS 11631
105	,,	,,	16115	,,	1933 LMS 11632
106	,,	,,	16116	,,	1931 LMS 11633 R/27 LY
107	,,	,,	16117	,,	1929 LMS 11634
3	D4	,,	17840	1907	1930 LMS 12480 R/26 LY
4	,,	,,	17841	,,	1930 LMS 12481

No.	Class	Builders	Date	Withdrawn	Notes
26	D1	,, 2279	1873	1930	R/16 T4 59 (1913) 63 (1918) LMS 12066
76	,,	,, 2280	,,	1925	R/01 T2 LMS 12006
77	,,	,, 2283	,,	1914	
78	,,	,, 2284	,,	1915	R/99 T2
79	,,	,, 2285	,,	1930	R/16 T4 LMS 12067
80	,,	,, 2316	,,	1916	
81	,,	,, 2317	,,	1921	R/00 T2
82	G1	,, 2300	,,	1925	LMS 11551
83	,,	,, 2301	,,	1925	LMS 11552
84	D1	,, 2337	,,	1915	
85	,,	,, 2338	,,	1925	R/00 T2 LMS 12009
86	,,	,, 2340	,,	1925	R/98 T2 LMS 12010
87	,,	,, 2341	,,	1924	R/98 T2 LMS 12011
5	E2	,, 2364	,,	1907	
6	,,	,, 2365	,,	1907	
11	,,	,, 2366	,,	1916	3 (1899) 3A (1907)
12	,,	,, 2367	,,	1920	4 (1899) 4A (1907)
92	D1	,, 2422	1874	1924	R/97 T2 75 (1914) LMS 12012
93	,,	,, 2423	,,	1925	R/99 T2 77 (1914) LMS 12013
94	C1	,, 2448	,,	1914	94A (1912)
95	,,	,, 2449	,,	1916	95A (1912)
96	,,	,, 2450	,,	1916	96A (1907)
97	,,	,, 2451	,,	1924	97A (1907) LMS 11258
88	D1	,, 2506	1875	1926	R/11 T3 LMS 12068
89	,,	,, 2507	,,	1926	R/12 T3 LMS 12069
90	,,	,, 2508	,,	1930	R/18 T4 LMS 12070
91	,,	,, 2509	,,	1924	R/00 T2 Dept. No. 1 (1918)
98	G2	RS 1008	1855 Ex WCE 1	1895	
99	,,	,, 1009	,, ,, ,, 2	1886	
100	,,	FJ 21	1858 ,, ,, 4	1918	100A (1904)
101	,,	RS 1310	1860 ,, ,, 5	1890	
102	,,	,, 1437	1862 ,, ,, 6	1900	
103	,,	,, 1487	1863 ,, ,, 7	1887	
104	,,	,, 1488	,, ,, ,, 8	1914	104A (1904)
105	,,	,, 1798	1867 ,, ,, 9	1921	105A (1904)
106	,,	,, 1804	1869 ,, ,, 10	1918	106A (1904)
107	,,	,, 1960	1870 ,, ,, 11	1918	107A (1904)
108	H1	SL	1850 Ex WCE 12	1898	
109	G2	RS 1997	1871 ,, ,, 13	1925	109A (1907) LMS 11547
110	,,	,, 2109	1873 ,, ,, 14	1920	110A (1907)
111	,,	,, 2110	,, ,, ,, 15	1920	111A (1907)
112	G3	AB 154	1875 ,, ,, 17	1925	108 (1904) 108A (1907) LMS 11548
113	G4	H 989	1857 ,, ,, 3	1898	
114	D1	SS 2945	1881	1926	R/10 T3. 115 (1898) 70 (1920) LMS 12071
115	,,	,, 2946	,,	1892	(Lindal subsidence)
116	,,	,, 2947	,,	1925	R/01 T2. 71 (1920) LMS 12014
117	,,	,, 2948	,,	1927	R/13 T3. 72 (1920) LMS 12072

5	,,	NBL	17842	1907	1934		LMS	12482	R/26 LY
6	,,	,,	17843	,,	1930		LMS	12483	R/26 LY
96	L3	,,	17808	,,	1938	LMS	11635	R/27 LY	
97	,,	,,	17809	,,	1941	LMS	11636	R/27 LY	
108	,,	,,	17810	,,	1935	LMS	11637		
109	,,	,,	17811	,,	1933	LMS	11638		
110	,,	,,	17812	,,	1931	LMS	11639		
111	,,	,,	17813	,,	1933	LMS	11640		
19	G5	VF	2523	1910	1942	55 (1918)	LMS	11553	
20	,,	,,	2524	,,	1930	56 (1918)	LMS	11554	
21	,,	,,	2525	,,	1930	57 (1918)	LMS	11555	
22	,,	,,	2526	,,	1932	58 (1918)	LMS	11556	
23	,,	,,	2527	,,	1932	59 (1918)	LMS	11557	
24	,,	,,	2528	,,	1935	60 (1918)	LMS	11558	
94	L4	K	4855	1912	1934	LMS	11641		
95	,,	,,	4856	,,	1929	LMS	11642		
130	K4	NBL	20071	1913	1932	LMS	10185		
131	,,	,,	20072	,,	1932	LMS	10186		
1	D5	,,	20073	,,	1956	LMS	12494		
2	,,	,,	20074	,,	1932	LMS	12495		
25	,,	,,	20075	,,	1932	LMS	12496		
26	,,	,,	20076	,,	1935	LMS	12497		
27	,,	,,	20865	1914	1932	LMS	12498		
28	,,	,,	20866	,,	1957	LMS	12499		
132	K4	,,	20867	,,	1932	LMS	10187		
133	,,	,,	20868	,,	1932	LMS	10188		
92	L4	K	5042	,,	1934	LMS	11643		
93	,,	,,	5043	,,	1932	LMS	11644		
38	M1	,,	5119	1915	1930	LMS	11080		
39	,,	,,	5120	,,	1932	LMS	11081		
51	G5	,,	5121	,,	1934	LMS	11559		
52	,,	,,	5122	,,	1930	LMS	11560		
53	,,	VF	3174	1916	1936	LMS	11561		
54	,,	,,	3175	,,	1931	LMS	11562		
40	M1	,,	3176	,,	1930	LMS	11082		
41	,,	,,	3177	,,	1932	LMS	11083		
42	,,	K	5172	,,	1930	LMS	11084		
43	,,	,,	5173	,,	1931	LMS	11085		
19	D5	,,	5195	1918	1932	LMS	12500		
20	,,	,,	5196	,,	1957	LMS	12501		
21	,,	,,	5197	,,	1930	LMS	12502		
22	,,	,,	5198	,,	1930	LMS	12503		
23	,,	NBL	21993	,,	1932	LMS	12504		
24	,,	,,	21994	,,	1932	LMS	12505		
29	,,	,,	21995	,,	1930	LMS	12506		
30	,,	,,	21996	,,	1935	LMS	12507		
31	,,	,,	22572	1920	1950	LMS	12508		
32	,,	,,	22573	,,	1956	LMS	12509		
33	,,	,,	22574	,,	1957	LMS	12510		
34	,,	,,	22575	,,	1932	LMS	12511		
35	,,	,,	22576	,,	1932	LMS	12512		
115	N1	K	5292	,,	1935	LMS	11100		
116	,,	,,	5293	,,	1935	LMS	11101		

11

No.	Class	Builders	Date	Withdrawn	Notes	
117	,,	,,	5294	,,	1934	LMS 11102
118	,,	,,	5295	,,	1940	LMS 11103
119	,,	,,	5296	1921	1935	LMS 11104

BUILDERS:—
BCK — Bury, Curtis & Kennedy, Liverpool.
AB — Andrew Barclay, Sons & Co., Kilmarnock.
EBW — E. B. Wilson, Leeds.
F — William Fairbairn & Co., Manchester.
FJ — Fletcher, Jennings & Co., Whitehaven.
H — R. & W. Hawthorn, Newcastle-on-Tyne.
K — Kitson & Co., Leeds.
N — Neilson & Co., Glasgow.
NBL — North British Locomotive Co., Glasgow.
NW — Nasmyth, Wilson & Co., Manchester.
RS — Robert Stephenson & Co., Darlington.
SL — Stothert & Slaughter, Bristol.
SB — Sharp Brothers, Manchester.
SS — Sharp, Stewart & Co., Manchester.
VF — Vulcan Foundry, Newton-le-Willows.
R/oo — denotes rebuilding date, last two figures being the year. In connection with this, T2, T3, T4 denote the type of boiler fitted at rebuilding to the D1 class 0–6–0's, and LY denotes fitted with L. & Y.R. saturated Belpaire boilers at Horwich Works, (D3 and D4 0–6–0's; L2 and L3 0–6–2 tanks.)
Renumberings are shown by the new number followed by the year in brackets, thus—32A (1896).

No drawings are given for Classes A1, A4, B2, and C2. The first three of these are well enough illustrated by A2, A3, and B3, respectively, since the differences were only minor. Class C2 cannot be illustrated, since the only known photograph of one of these engines is far too poor for any useful purpose.

Class	Date	Type	Wheels			Cyls	Wheelbase	Boiler					Heating Surface			Grate Area	Tractive Effort	Weight (W.O.)	Water	Coal	Tender Weight
			Driving	Leading	Trailing			Diam	Length	Pitch	Pressure	Tubes	Tubes	Firebox	Total						
A1	1844	0.4.0	4'9"	-	-	13x24	7'5"	3'9"	10'0"	6'0"	90	132x2"	691.4	49.0	740.4	9.0	5443	17-15	900	2	13-15
A2	1846	"	4'9"	-	-	14x24	7'5"	3'10"	10'0"	6'0"	110	146x2"	805.0	49.0	854.0	9.0	7617	19-10	900	2	13-15
A3	1854	"	4'6"	-	-	15x24	7'9"	4'2"	10'8"	6'3"	120	148x2"	891.0	49.0	940.0	9.0	9350	21-9	1000	2	15-12
A4	1858	"	4'6"	-	-	15x24	7'9"	4'2"	10'8"	6'3"	120	148x2"	891.0	49.0	940.0	9.0	9350	24-4	1300	2	17-14
A5	1863	"	4'9"	-	-	15½x24	7'9"	4'2"	10'8"	6'2"	120	150x2"	870.0	56.0	926.0	9.2	10317	24-18	1500	2	19-15
B1	1851	2.2.2T	5'6"	3'6"	3'6"	14x18	7'3"+7'3"	4'0"	9'8"	5'9"	120	154x2"	780.0	55.0	835.0	9.0	7121	30-5	560	1¼	-
B2	1857	"	5'6"	3'6"	3'6"	14x20	7'0"+7'3"	4'2"	9'7"	6'2"	120	154x2"	780.0	60.0	840.0	9.5	8057	30-2	560	1½	-
B3	1864	"	5'6"	3'6"	3'6"	15x18	7'3"+7'0"	4'2"	9'7"	6'1"	120	160x2"	788.0	80.0	868.0	11.5	7954	30-5	560	1¼	-
B4	1860	"	5'6"	3'6"	3'6"	14x20	5'9"+9'0"	3'10"	9'6"	5'9"	120	154x2"	753.0	47.0	800.0	9.0	6057	27-2	550	1½	-
B5	1850	"	5'3"	3'6"	3'6"	12x18	6'6"+6'8"	3'9"	8'6"	6'0"	120	154x2"	690.0	49.0	739.0	8.5	6460	27-0	500	1¼	-
C1	1864	0.4.0ST	4'0"	-	-	14x20	7'9"	3'5"	10'6"	5'10"	120	109x2"	613.5	55.5	669.0	9.9	8330	24-10	600	¾	-
C2	1862	"	4'0"	-	-	10x16															-
D1	1866	0.6.0	4'6½"	-	-	16x24	6'9"+8'0"	3'10"	10'4"	6'2"	120	180x1¾"	871.27	88.0	959.27	13.8	11605	30-19	1600	2½	20-0
Rebuilt	1898	"	4'6½"	-	-	16x24	6'9"+8'0"	4'3"	10'6"	6'6"	140	208x1¾"	1029.0	101.0	1130.0	15.9	13539	35-7	1600	2½	20-0
Rebuilt	1910	"	4'6½"	-	-	16x24	6'9"+8'0"	4'3"	10'0"	7'2"	160	208x1¾"	982.0	88.0	1070.0	15.4	15830	33-19	1600	2½	20-0
Rebuilt	1916	"	4'6½"	-	-	16x24	6'9"+8'0"	4'3"	9'10"	7'2"	150	208x1¾"	966.0	101.0	1067.0	15.9	14105	34-5	1600	2½	20-0
D2	1864	"	4'6"	-	-	16x24	6'0"+6'8"	4'2"	9'0"	6'2"	120	175x2"	846.0	72.0	918.0	11.5	11605	28-6	1600	3	18-11
D3	1899	"	4'7½"	-	-	18x26	7'9"+7'9"	4'3"	10'6"	7'3"	150	208x1¾"	1029.0	105.0	1134.0	20.5	19352	38-10	2500	3½	28-5
D4	1907	"	5'1"	-	-	18x26	7'9"+7'9"	4'3"	10'6"	7'9"	160	208x1¾"	1029.0	105.0	1134.0	20.5	18781	40-8	2500	3½	28-5
D5	1913	"	4'7½"	-	-	18x26	7'9"+7'9"	4'7"	10'6"	7'9"	170	230x1¾"	1139.0	107.0	1246.0	20.5	21938	44-17	3300	5	37-9
E1	1870	2.4.0	5'6"	3'6"	-	16x20	6'6"+8'6"	4'0"	9'9"	6'2"	120	183x1¾"	839.5	71.0	910.5	11.5	7913	30-5	1600	2½	20-0
F1	1857	0.4.2	5'0"	-	3'6"	14x20	7'6"+6'6"	3'11"	9'9"	5'9"	120	180x1¾"	849.5	57.5	907.0	11.0	6664	27-11	1500	2½	17-7
G1	1867	0.6.0T	4'6"	-	-	18x24	7'0"+8'6"	4'0"	10'0"	6'7"	140	193x2"	1016.0	95.0	1111.0	15.67	17136	44-14	1000	1½	-

Class	Date	Type	Wheels: Driving	Wheels: Leading	Wheels: Trailing	Cyls.	Wheelbase	Boiler: Diam.	Boiler: Length	Boiler: Pitch	Boiler: Pressure	Boiler: Tubes	Heating Surface: Tubes	Heating Surface: Firebox	Heating Surface: Total	Grate Area	Tractive Effort	Weight (W.O.)	Water	Coal	Tender Weight
G2	1855	0.6.0ST	4'6"	-	-	17x24	6'6"+7'9"	4'0"	10'9"	6'4"	150	186x1¾"	920.0	75.0	995.0	13.3	16376	44-0	1000	1¼	-
G3	1875	"	4'6"	-	-	17x24	6'6"+7'9"	4'0"	10'8"	6'4"	150	186x1¾"	922.0	70.0	992.0	13.5	16376	43-19	1000	1¼	-
G4	1857	0.6.0T	4'0"	-	-	14x22	5'8"+5'10"	4'0"	9'8"	6'0"	150	140x2"	718.0	69.0	787.0	10.8	8135	34-0	800	1¼	-
G5	1910	"	4'7½"	-	-	17½x24	7'4"+7'8"	4'3"	10'0"	7'6"	160	208x1¾"	982.0	88.0	1070.0	15.4	18011	48-17	1050	2	-
G5	1915	"	4'7½"	-	-	17½x24	7'4"+7'8"	4'3"	10'0"	7'8"	160	208x1¾"	982.0	88.0	1070.0	15.4	18011	49-10	1070	2¼	-
H1	1850	2.4.0T	5'0"	3'6"	-	15x20	6'0"+8'3"	4'0"	10'3"	6'2"	120	156x2"	840.0	71.0	911.0	11.0	8415	36-0	1000	1¼	-
J1	1891	2.4.2T	5'6"	3'6"	3'6"	16x20	6'6"+8'6"+6'6"	4'0"	9'9"	6'2"	140	183x1¾"	839.5	71.0	910.5	11.5	9233	44-11	1000	1¾	-
K1	1890	4.4.0	5'0"	3'0"	-	17x24	6'0"+6'6"+8'0"	4'2"	10'3"	6'10"	140	172x2"	955.0	86.0	1041.0	14.2	12412	36-2	2500	4	28-5
K2	1896	"	6'0"	3'0"	-	18x24	5'9"+6'8"+8'6"	4'2"	10'3"	7'1"	150	230x1¾"	1109.0	99.5	1208.5	17.0	13770	41-6	2500	3½	28-5
K3	1908	"	6'6"	3'6"	-	18x26	6'0"+7'3½"+8'6"	4'3"	10'8½"	7'5"	160	230x1¾"	1154.75	108.5	1263.25	17.75	14688	43-0	3000	5½	32-14
K4	1913	"	6'0"	3'6"	-	18x26	6'0"+7'3½"+8'6"	4'7"	10'0"	8'0"	170	230x1¾"	1086.0	107.0	1193.0	20.5	16906	46-12	3300	5	37-9
K4	1914	"	6'6"	3'6"	-	18x26	6'0"+7'3½"+8'6"	4'7"	10'6"	8'0"	170	230x1¾"	1139.0	107.0	1246.0	20.5	16906	47-12	3300	5	37-9
L1	1898	0.6.2T	4'7½"	-	3'8½"	18x26	7'5"+7'0"+6'3"	4'3"	10'6"	7'3"	140	208x1¾"	1029.0	105.0	1134.0	20.5	18062	54-14	1400	1½	-
L2	1904	"	5'1"	-	3'8½"	18x26	7'9"+8'6"+7'9"	4'3"	10'6"	7'9"	160	208x1¾"	1029.0	105.0	1134.0	20.5	18781	55-3	1700	2	-
L3	1907	"	5'1"	-	3'8½"	18x26	7'9"+8'6"+7'9"	4'3"	10'6"	7'9"	160	208x1¾"	1029.0	105.0	1134.0	20.5	18781	56-17	1700	3	-
L4	1912	"	4'7½"	-	3'8½"	18x26	7'5"+7'3"+6'3"	4'7"	9'3"	7'9"	170	208x1¾"	911.0	105.0	1016.0	20.5	21933	56-18	1150	2¼	-
L4	1914	"	4'7½"	-	3'8½"	18x26	7'5"+7'3"+6'3"	4'7"	10'6"	7'9"	170	230x1¾"	1139.0	107.0	1246.0	20.5	21933	58-12	1170	2¼	-
M1	1915	4.4.2T	5'8"	3'2"	3'9"	17½x24	6'0"+7'3½" +8'0"+7'9"	4'3"	10'0"	7'9"	160	208x1¾"	982.0	88.0	1070.0	15.4	14700	59-9	1750	3	-
M1	1916	"	5'8"	3'2"	3'9"	17½x24	6'0"+7'3½" +8'0"+7'9"	4'3"	10'0"	7'9"	160	220x1¾"	1039.0	88.0	1127.0	15.4	14700	59-9	1750	3	-
N1	1920	4.6.4T	5'8"	3'2"	3'2"	19½x26	7'0"+6'9"+6'7½" +6'7½"+6'9"+7'0"	5'0"	15'0"	8'9"	170	230x2	1850.0	153.0	2003.0	26.0	21008	92-15	2200	4	-
RM	1905	0.4.0T	2'10"	-	3'9"	11x14	8'0"+31'6"+8'0"	4'0"	3'6"	7'9"	160	226x1¾"	438.4	71.0	509.4	12.0	6776	43-10	500	¾	-

LOCOMOTIVES

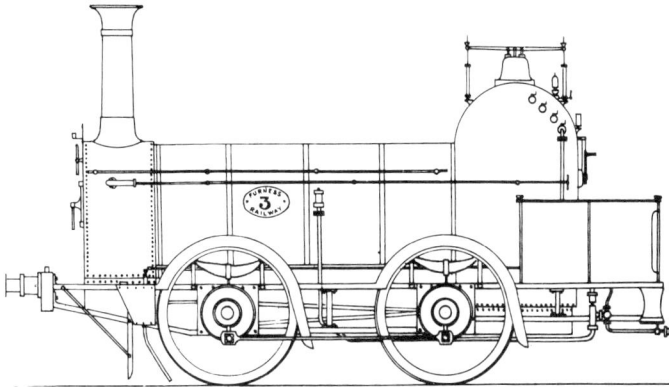

1. 0-4-0   Class A2, No.3

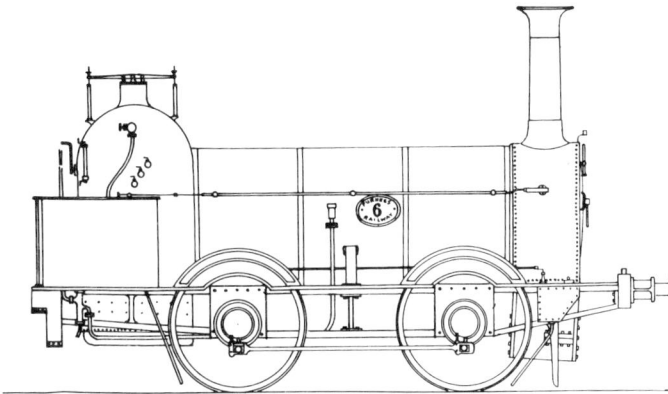

2. 0-4-0   Class A3, No.6

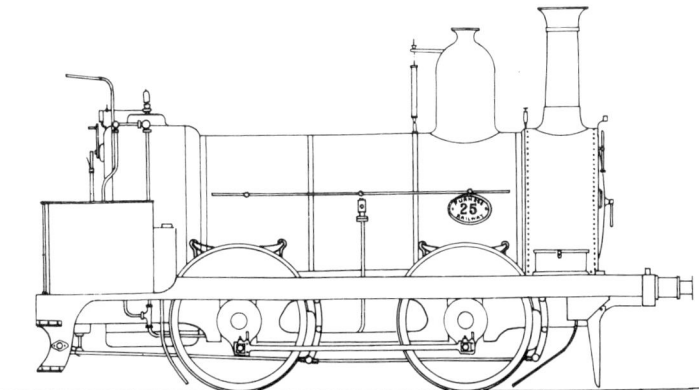

3. 0-4-0   Class A5, No.25

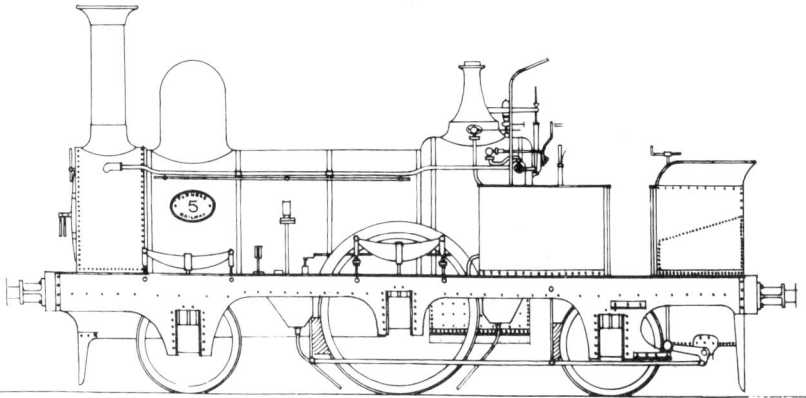

4.   2-2-2T   Class B1, No.5

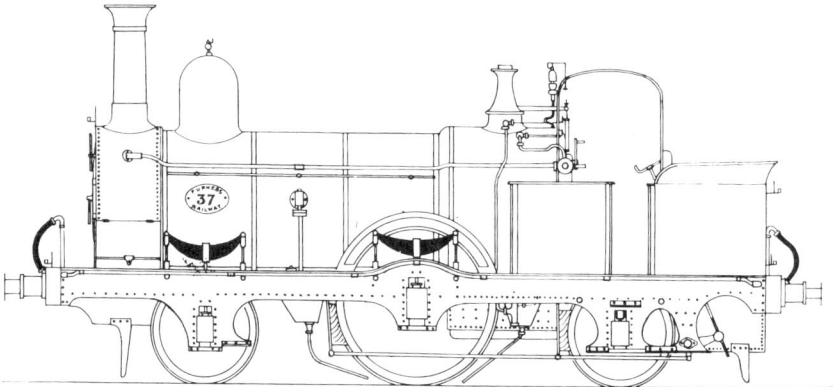

5.   2-2-2T   Class B3, No.37

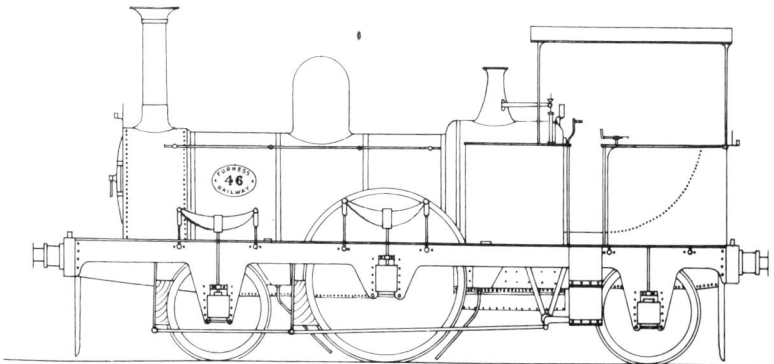

6.   2-2-2T   Class B4. Ex-W.F.J.R. "Queen Mab"

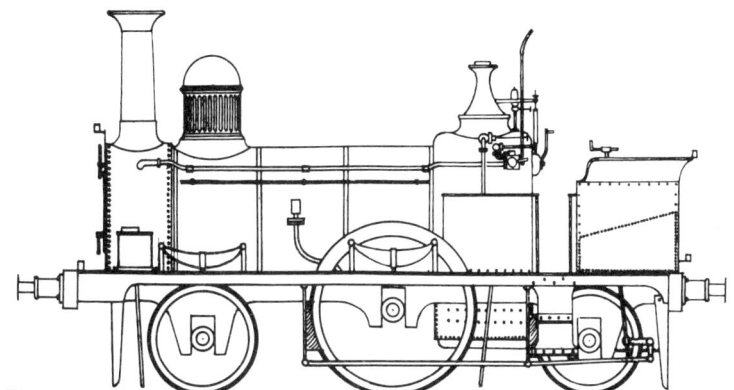

7.   2-2-2T   Class B5, Ex-W.F.J.R. "Oberon"

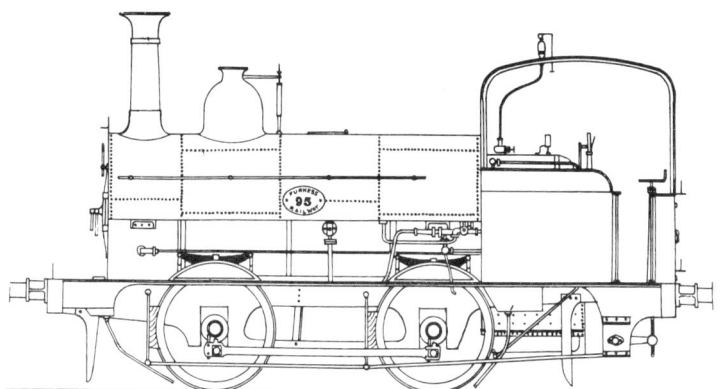

8.   0-4-0ST   Class C1, No.95

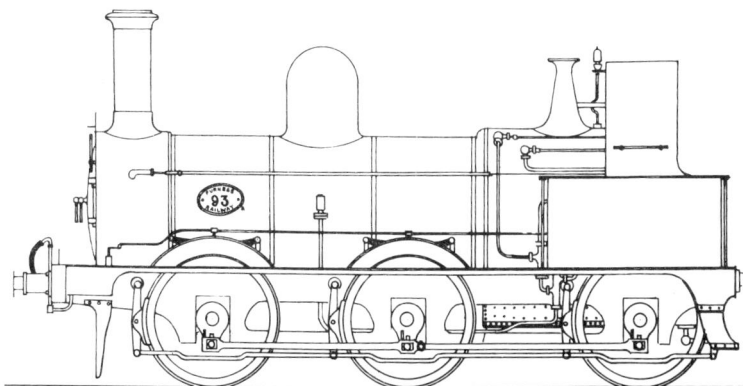

9.   0-6-0   Class D1, No.93, as built

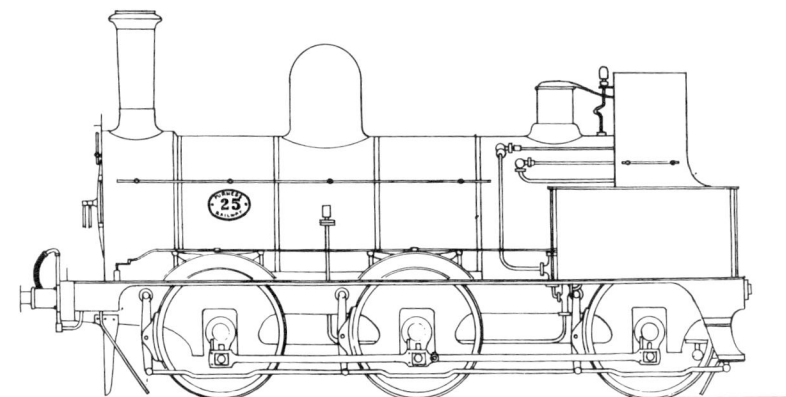

10. 0-6-0 Class D1, No.25, rebuilt Type 2 boiler

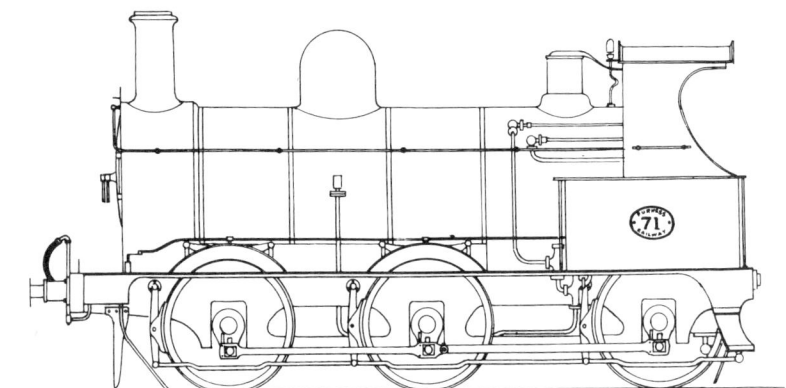

11. 0-6-0 Class D1, No.71, rebuilt Type 3 boiler

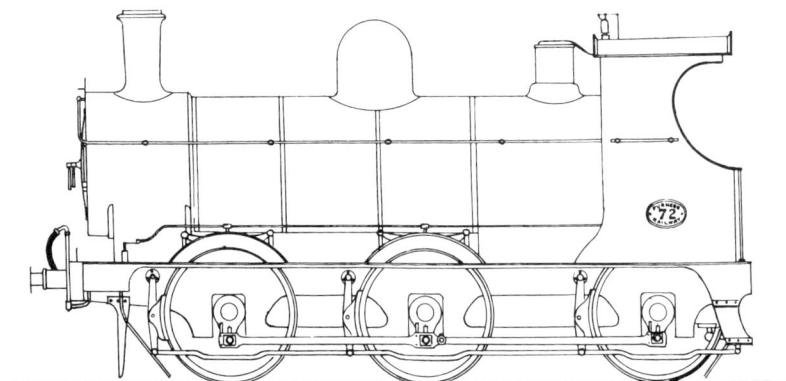

12. 0-6-0 Class D1, No.72, rebuilt Type 4 boiler

13.   0-6-0   Class D2, No.42, Ex-W.F.J.R. "Lonsdale"

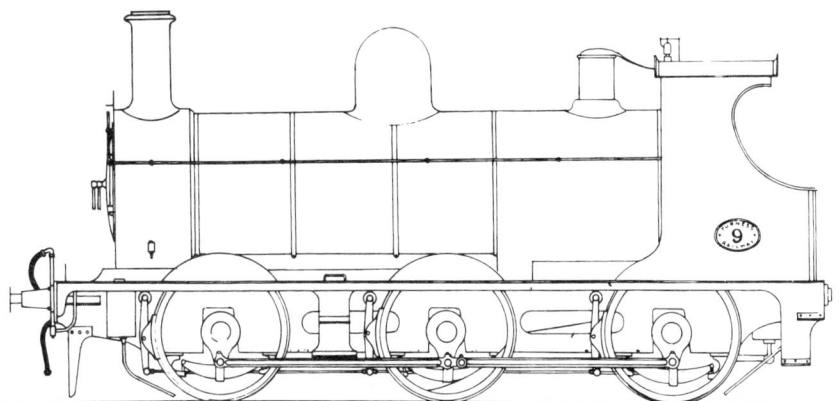

14.   0-6-0   Class D3, No.9

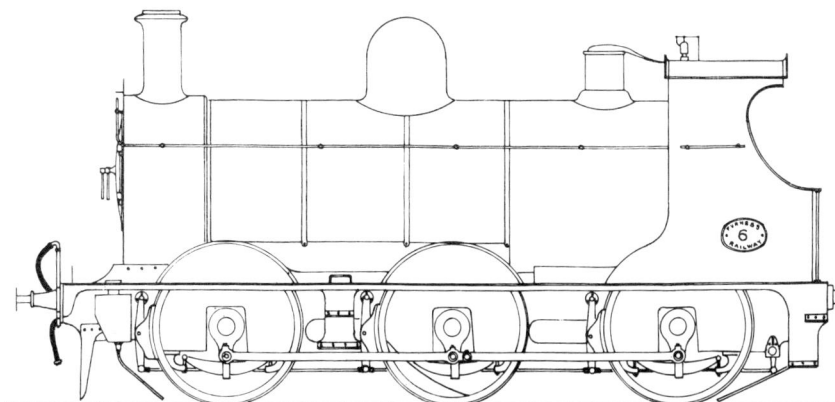

15.   0-6-0   Class D4, No.6

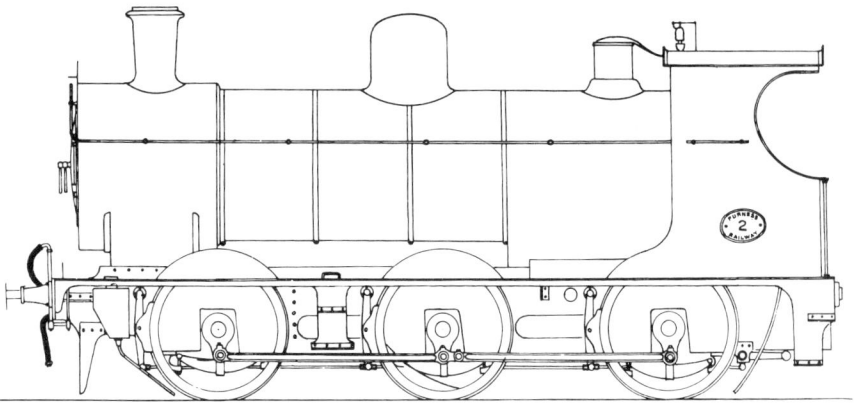

16. 0-6-0   Class D5, No.2

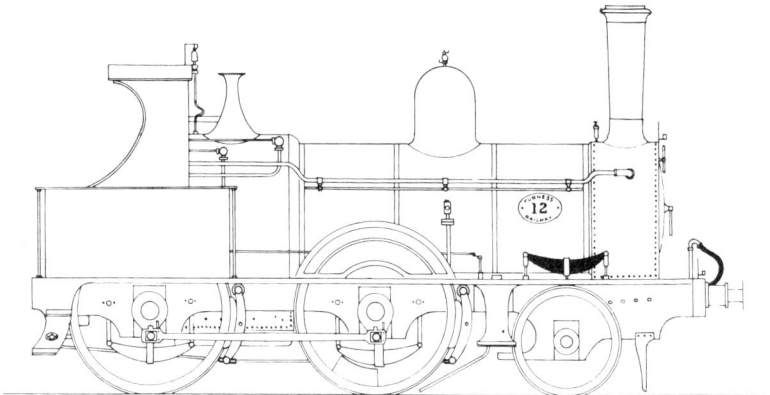

17. 2-4-0   Class E1, No.12

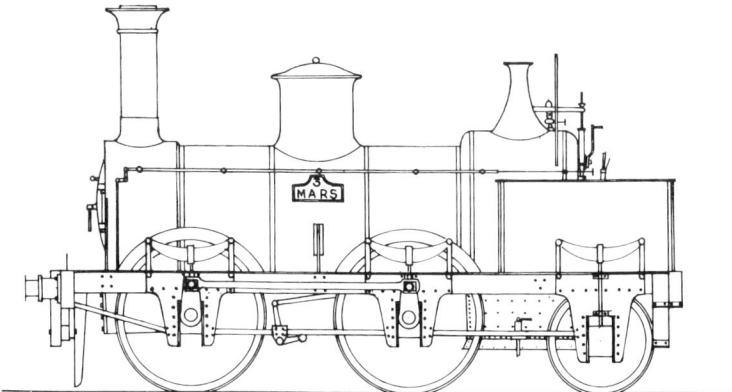

18. 0-4-2   Class F1, No.44, Ex-W.F.J.R. "Mars"

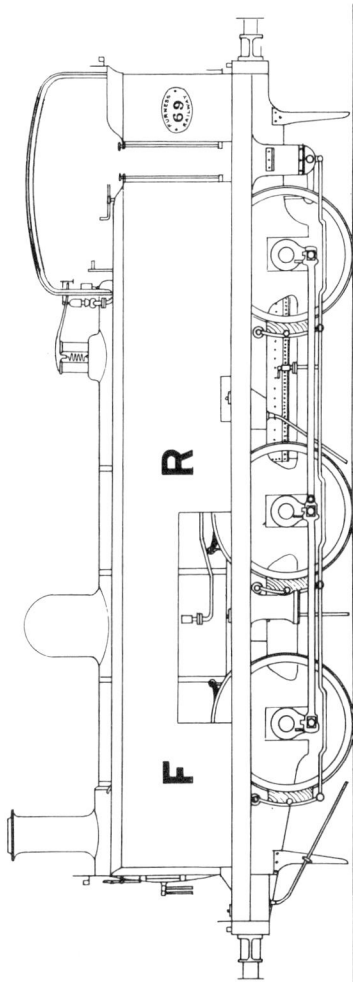

19. 0-6-0T   Class G1, No.69

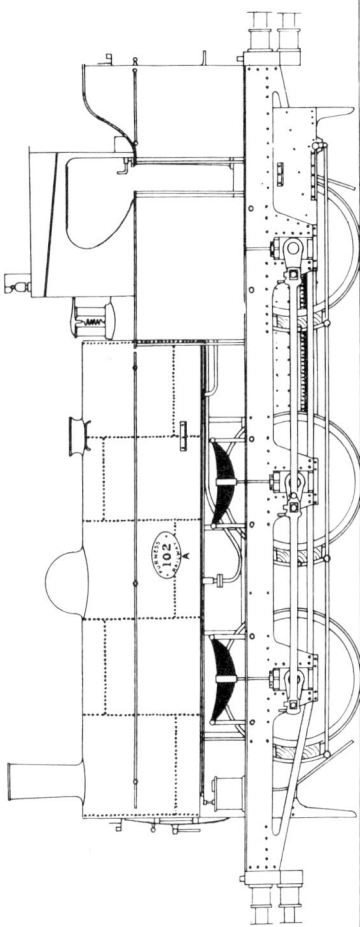

20. 0-6-0ST   Class G2, No.102, Ex-W.C.E.R. "Parkside"

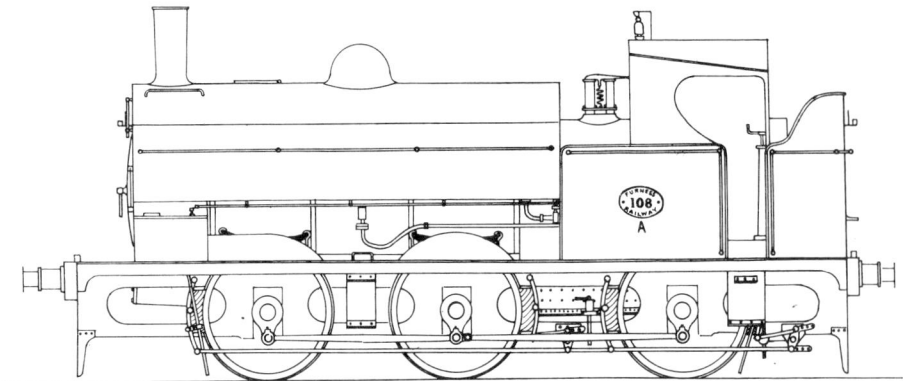

21.   0-6-0ST   Class G3, No.108, Ex-W.C.E.R. "Wastwater"

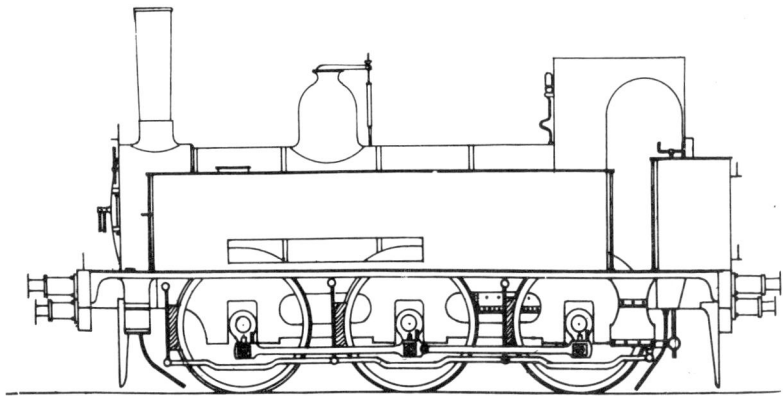

22.   0-6-0T   Class G4, No.113, Ex-W.C.E.R. "Victoria"

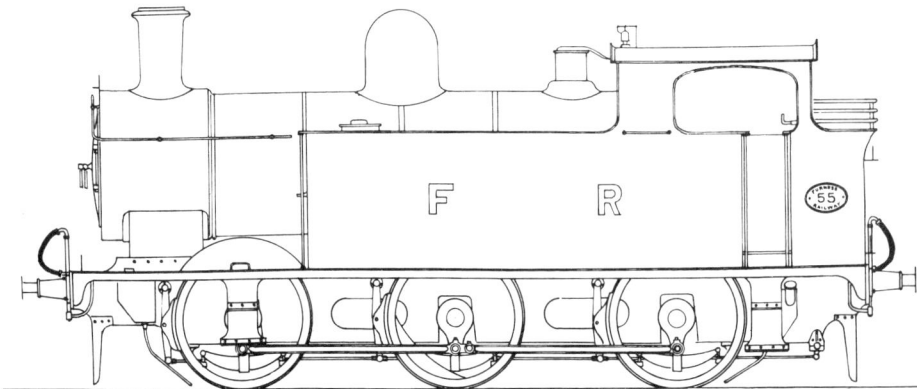

23.   0-6-0T   Class G5, No.55

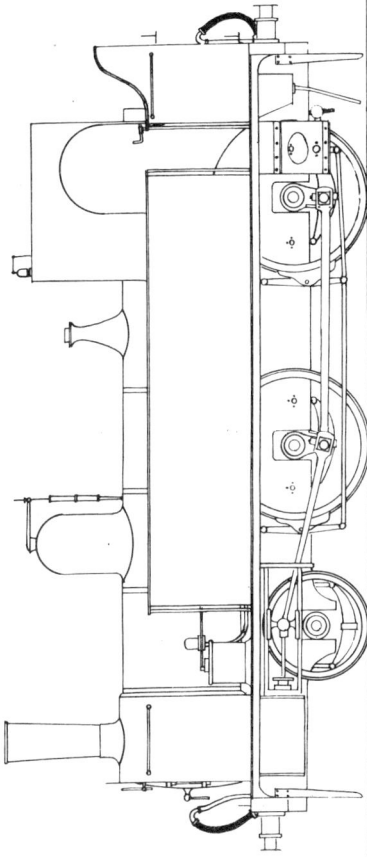

24. 2-4-0 Class H1, No.108, Ex-W.C.E.R. "Marron"

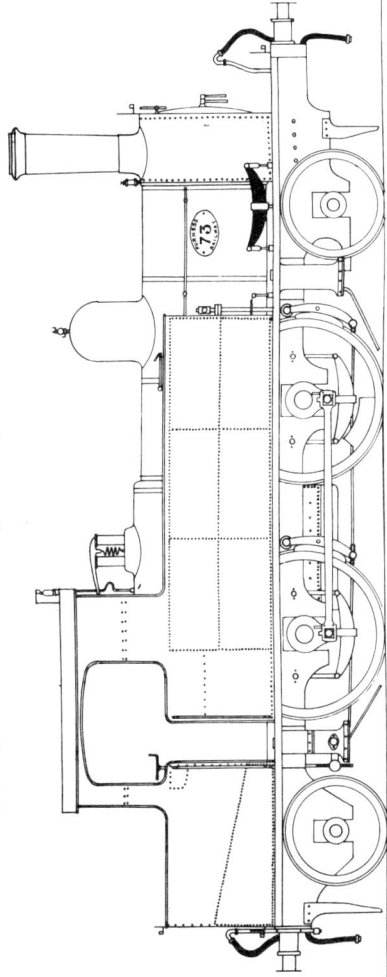

25. 2-4-2T Class J1, No.73, rebuilt from Class E1

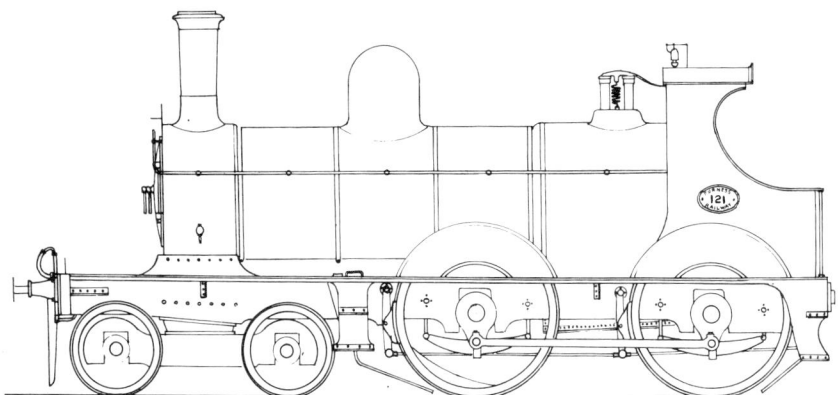

26.   4-4-0   Class K1, No.121

27.   4-4-0   Class K2, No.46

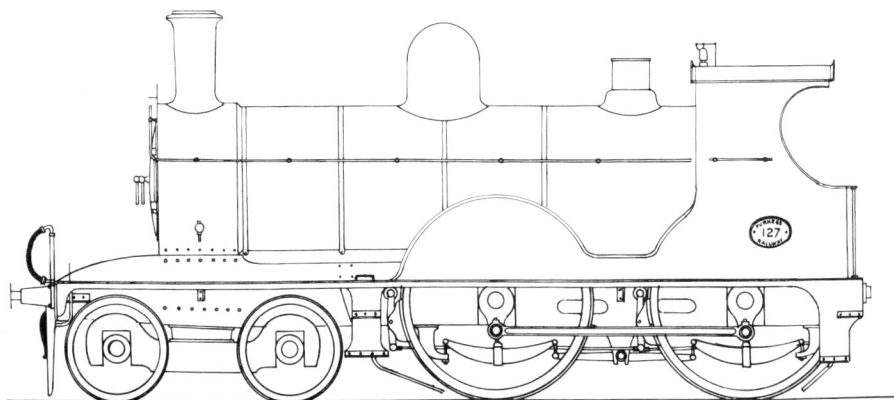

28.   4-4-0   Class K3, No.127

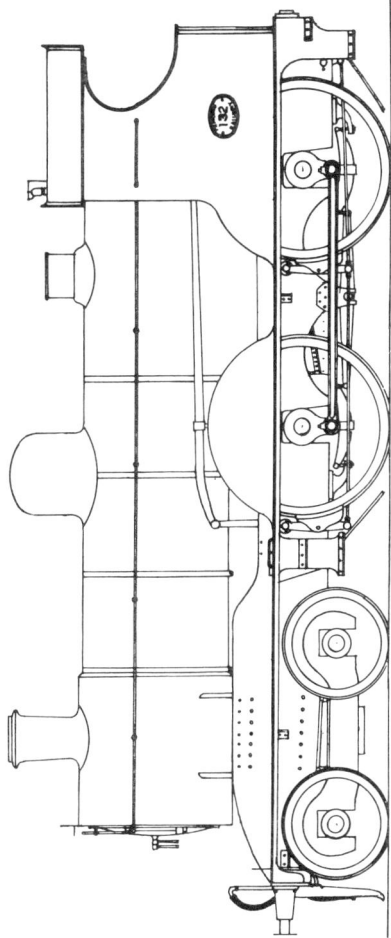

29.   4-4-0   Class K4, No.132

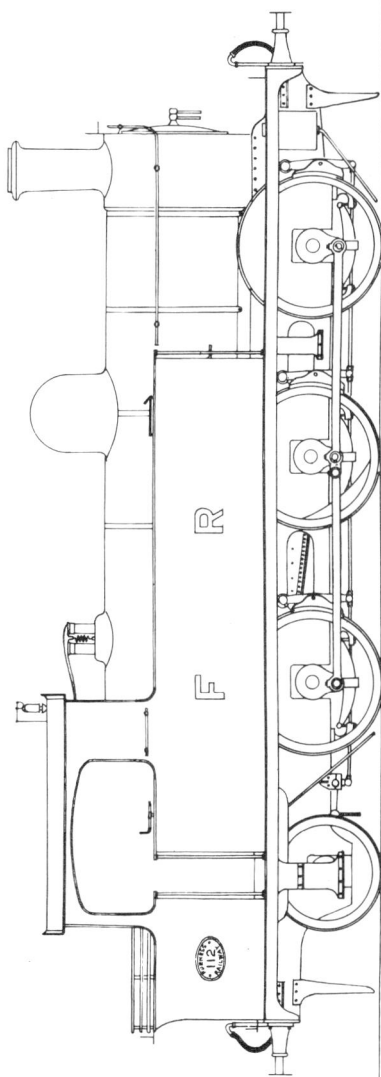

30.   0-6-2T   Class L1, No.112

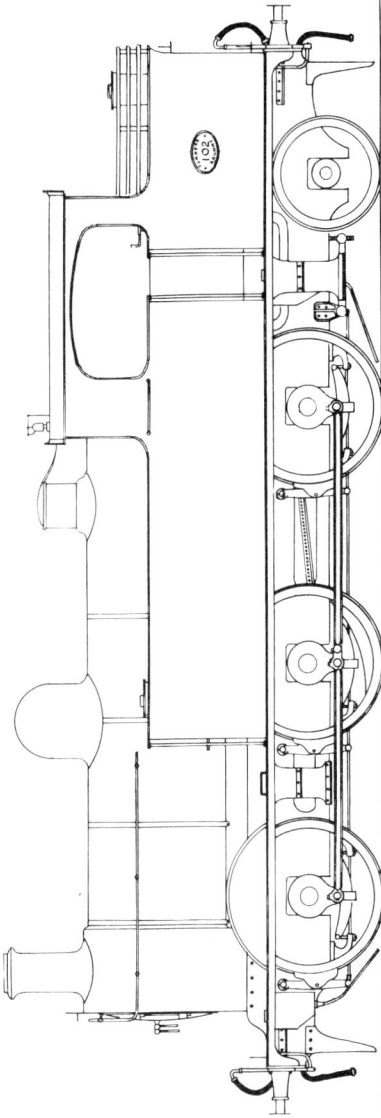

31. 0-6-2T   Class L2, No.102

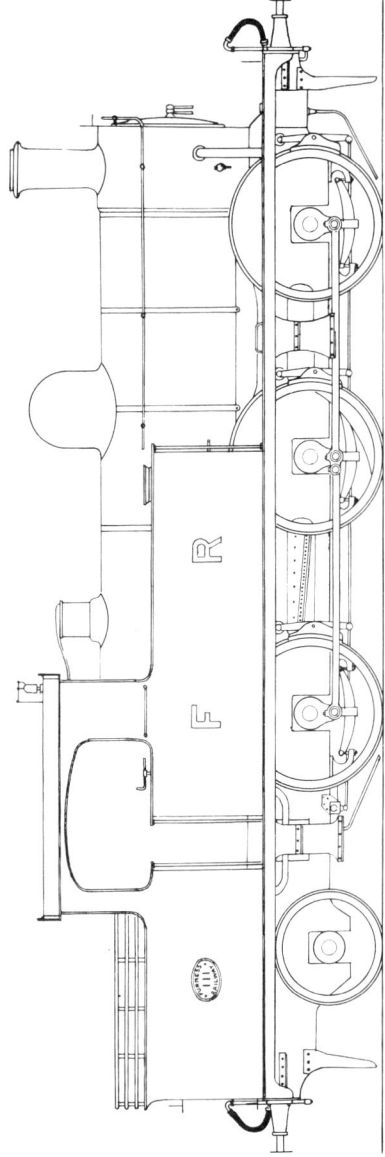

32. 0-6-2T   Class L3, No.111

F R

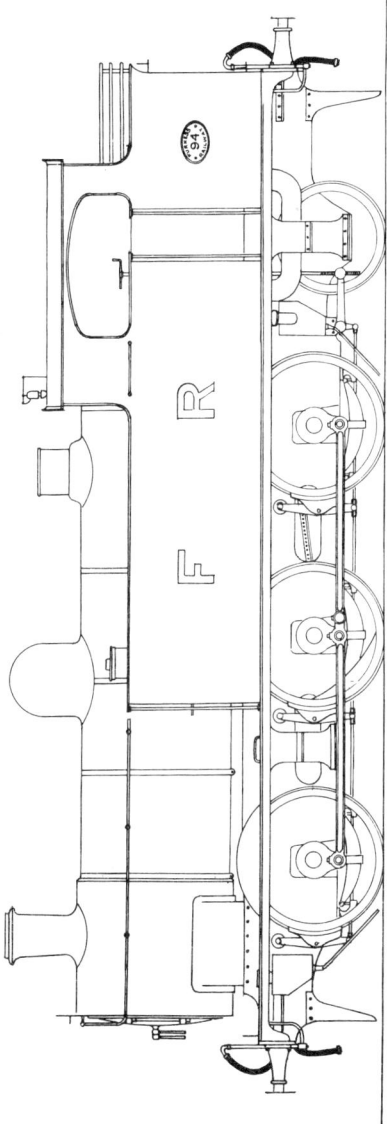

33.   0-6-2T   Class L4, No.94

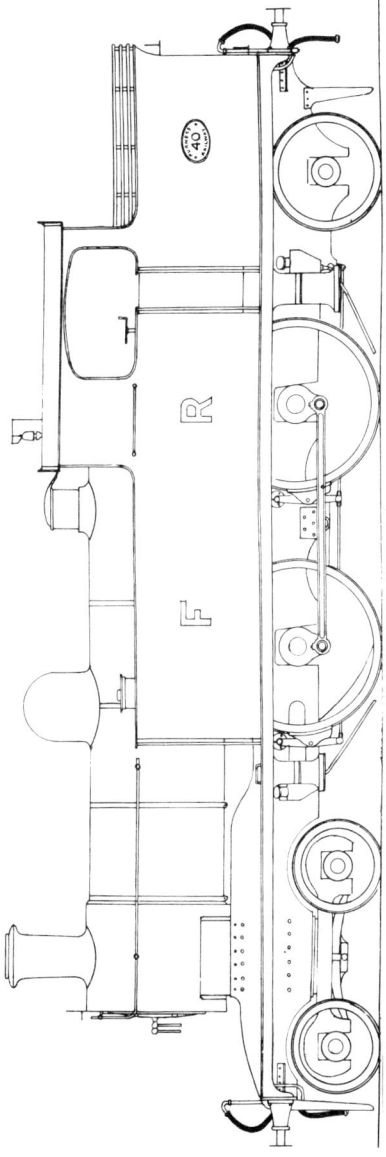

F R

34.   4-4-2T   Class M1, No.40

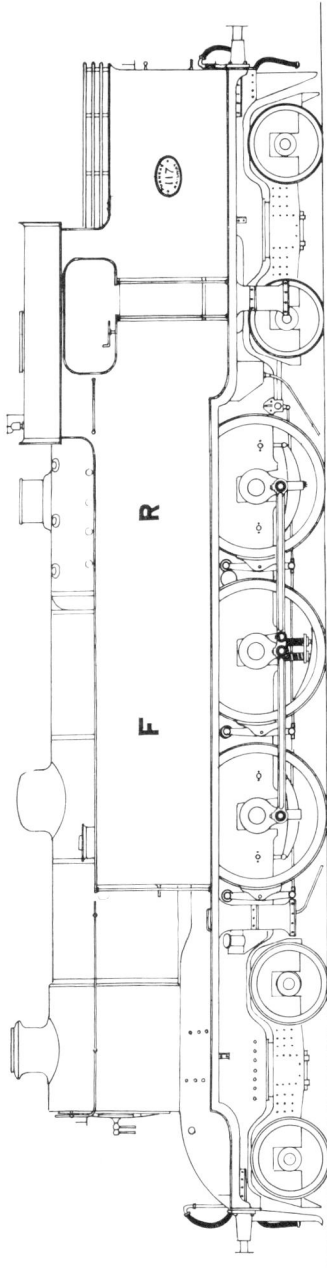

35. 4-6-4T   Class N1, No.117

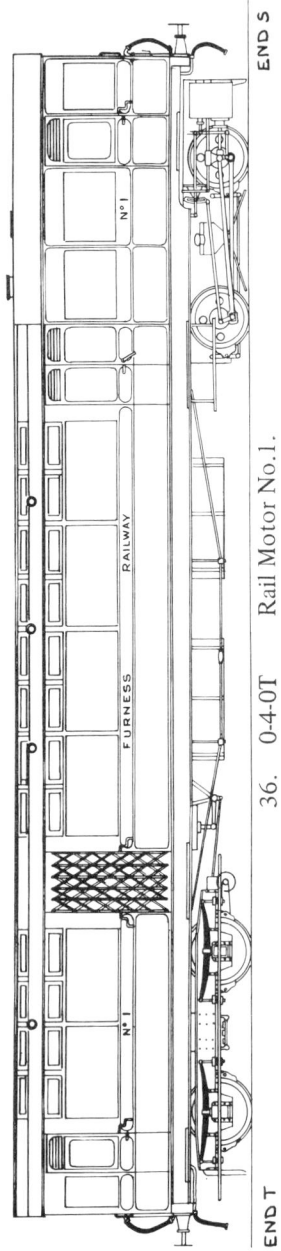

F R

36. 0-4-0T   Rail Motor No.1.

FURNESS RAILWAY

N°1

N°1

END T

END S

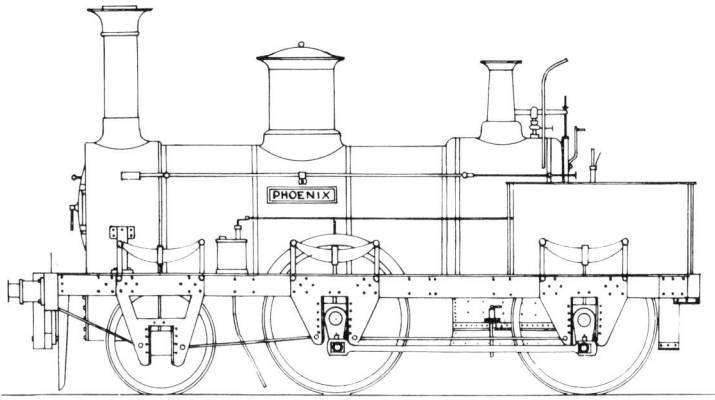

37.   2-4-0   "Phoenix", W.F.J.R.

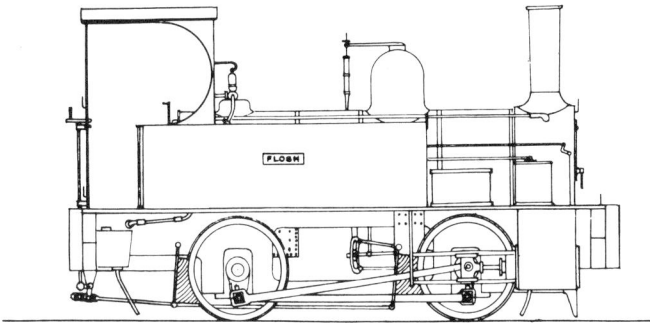

38.   0-4-0T   "Flosh", C. & W.R.

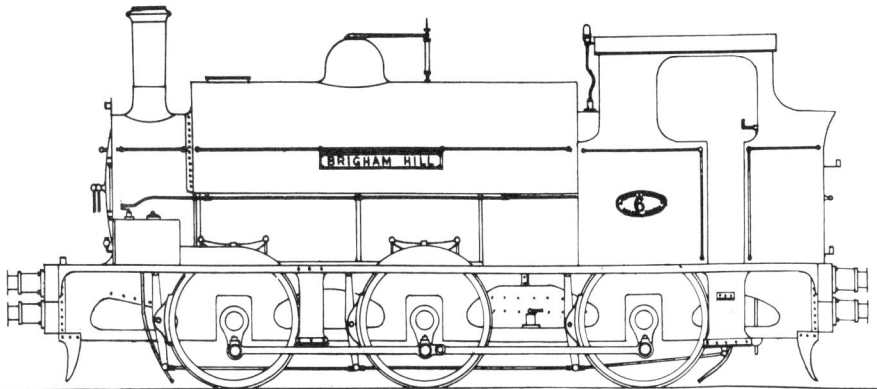

39.   0-6-0ST   "Brigham Hill", C. & W.R. No.6

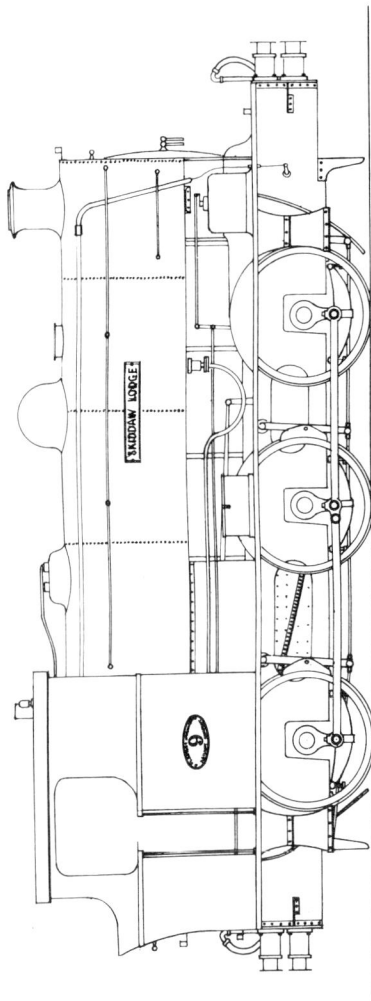

40.   0-6-0ST   "Skiddaw Lodge", C. & W.R. No.9

PASSENGER STOCK

F.R. Diag.	Arrangement	Dimensions	Wheels	Date & No. Built	L.M.S. Nos. 1923	L.M.S. Nos. 1933
1.	333333333	57' 0" x 9' 0"	8	1919 (2)	15146/7	15326/7
				1920 (9)	15148–56	15328–36
				1921 (1)	15157	15337
2.	33333333	49' 0" x 8' 6"	8	1912 (4)	15130–3	15309–12
				1913 (4)	15134–7	15313–6
				1914 (6)	15106/38–42	15317–22
				1915 (3)	15143–5	15323–5
3.	33333333	48' 0" x 8' 6"	8	1902 (12)	15107–18	15297–308
4.	33333	30'9¾" x 8' 0"	6	1893 (49)	15187–274,	26653–701
				1894 (1)	Except	27796–9, (a)
				1896 (24)	15237–40 &	27425 (b)
				1897 (6)	15254	
				1898 (2)		
4A.	3333333	40' 0" x 8' 6"	8	1902 (1)	15119	15295
				1903 (1)	15120	15296
5.	33333	30'9¾" x 8' 0"	6	1891 (21)	15275–300	26638–50
				1892 (4)	15018/9	26651
					15104/5	26652
6.	33L33	30'9¾" x 8' 0"	6	1894 (4)	15237–40	26636/7
						(ex 15237/9)
7.	333333	34'3¾" x 8' 0"	6	1884 (1)	?	–
8.	3333	25' 0" x 7' 9"	4	1882(?)	?	–
9.	33T333T33	49' 0" x 8' 6"	8	1904 (4)	15126–9	18926–9
10.	333T3333	43' 6" x 8' 0"	8	1903 (1)	15121	18921
				1906 (2)	15122/3	18922/3
				1907 (2)	15124/5	18924/5
11.	3333Gd	49' 0" x 8' 6"	8	1908 (5)	15050–4	24150–4
				1909 (1)	15059	24155
				1915 (2)	15060/1	24156/7
12.	3333Gd	49' 0" x 8' 6"	8	1906 (1)	15055	24146
				1907 (3)	15056–8	24147–9
13.	333333Gd	48' 0" x 8' 6"	8	1901 (3)	15068–70	24138–40
				1902 (5)	15071–5	24141–5
14.	333Gd	30'9¾" x 8' 0"	6	1894 (3)	15062–4	27796
				1895 (3)	15065–7	27793–5
15.	33Gd	25' 0" x 7' 9"	4	1882 (?)	?	–
16.	T3333333T	49' 0" x 8' 6"	8	1904 (1)	15014	3314
				1905 (1)	15015	3315
				1914 (2)	15016/7	3316/7
17.	T1111333T	57' 0" x 9' 0"	8	1921 (1)	15024	4947
				1922 (1)	15025	4948
				1923 (2)	15026/7	4949/50
				1924 (2)	15028/9	4951/2
18.	T1113333T	49' 0" x 8' 6"	8	1906 (2)	15020/1	4943/4
				1915 (2)	15022/3	4945/6
19.	3311 T/T 133	49' 0" x 8' 6"	8	1903 (6)	15172–7	19936–41
20.	11 T/T 33L	35' 0" x 8' 6"	6	1900 (1)	15036	–
				1901 (1)	15037	27456
21.	3333 T/T 11L	47' 0" x 8' 0"	8	1897 (6)	15030–5	19933/4/0/1, 19935/2 (c)
22.	333 T/T 11Gd	47' 0" x 8' 0"	8	1897 (6)	15009–13	25946–51
					15254	
23.	331133Gd	48' 0" x 8' 6"	8	1901 (1)	15042	24768
				1902 (7)	15043–9	24769–75

F.R. Diag.	Arrangement	Dimensions	Wheels	Date & No. Built	L.M.S. Nos. 1923	1933
24.	3113Gd	34'3¾" x 8' 0"	6	1888 (2)	15040/1	27961(ex15041)
				1889 (2)	15038/9	27960(ex15038)
25.	31L13	33'9¾" x 8' 6"	6	1890 (4)	15162–5	27227/8
						(ex 15162/3)
				1891 (8)	15158–61,	27229–31
					15166–9	(ex 15158/67/8)
				1892 (1)	15170	–
				1899 (1)	15171	–
26.	331133	39' 0" x 8' 6"	6	1882 (6)	?	–
27.	S 3 L	42' 0" x 8' 6"	8	1900 (2)	15005/6	969 (ex 15006)
28.	GdTS 1 S 1	42' 0" x 7' 9"	8	1889 (1)	15001	821
29.	S 3	39' 0" x 8' 6"	6	1882 (1)	15004/5	– (d)
30.	Gd S1 T S1	34' 6" x 8' 0"	6	1891 (1)	15003	968
31.	S 3 L	32' 0" x 8' 0"	6	1875 (1)	15002	– (e)
32.	GPO Van	32' 0" x 8' 0"	6	1903 (1)		
33.	GPO Van	22' 6" x 8' 0"	6	1887 (1)		
34.	PBV	34' 0" x 8' 0"	6	1898 – 1905 (10)		
35.	PBV	30' 0" x 8' 0"	6	1897 (1) 1898 (1)		
36.	PBV	25' 6" x 7' 9"	4	1883 (6) 1885 (2) 1886 (4)		
37.	Horse Box	21' 0" x 8' 0"	4	1897 (6)		
38.	Horse Box	17' 0" x 7' 7"	4	1880 – 1904 (16)		
39.	Carr. Truck	21' 0" x 8' 0"	4	1889 – 1904 (9)		
40.	Fish Truck	18' 0" x 7' 6"	4	1891/2 (16)		
41.	Ventilated Van	18' 0" x 8' 0"	4	1899 – 1901 (4)		
42.	Prize Cattle Van	18' 0" x 8' 0"	4	1898 (1)		
43.	Carr. Van	22' 0" x 8' 0"	4	1907 (3)		

NOTES:

T = Lavatory.   L = Luggage compartment.   Gd = Guard's van.   S = Saloon
PBV = Passenger brake van.
Figures underlined, or overlined (e.g. $\overline{333T}$) denote corridor. (Note, there were no vehicles with central gangways.)
$\frac{T}{T}$= two lavatories side by side, usually for different classes.

(a) Nos. 27796-9 were converted to brake thirds after the grouping.
(b) No. 27425 had been altered to 33T33 after the grouping.
(c) Nos. 19933-5 were altered to four firsts and two thirds after the grouping.
(d) Rebuilt from Cleminson composites (Diagram 26) in 1893.
(e) Rebuilt from composite (31133) in 1891.

Diagrams 4 and 5, the five-compartment six wheeled thirds, were a complicated problem. Incidentally, the only difference between them was in the arrangement of the outside panelling. Taking Diagram 5 first, it will be seen from the table that in 1923, thirty L.M.S. numbers were allotted to only 25 vehicles, so there must have been five blanks, but what these were exactly is a matter of conjecture; Also, for some reason unknown, four of them, 15018/9, 15104/5, were entirely out of series. By 1933 the total had been whittled down to 15, which received the new series numbers 26638–52. The corresponding 1923 and 1933 numbering was as follows: –

1933.	1923.	Built.	1933.	1923.	Built.
26638	15275	1891	26646	15291	1891
26639	15277	,,	26647	15293	,,
26640	15278	,,	26648	15295	,,
26641	15281	,,	26649	15298	,,
26642	15285	,,	26650	15300	,,
26643	15286	,,	26651	15019	1892
26644	15287	,,	26652	15104	,,
26645	15289	,,			

Thus between 1923 and 1933, the following numbers had disappeared – 15276/9/80/2/3/4/8/90/2/4/6/7/9, 15018, 15105. Of those between 15276 and 15299, five must have been originally left blank, but which it is impossible to say.

Turning to Diagram 4, the position here was more complicated. 82 coaches were built to this diagram, with 83 numbers allotted in 1923, 15187–236/41–53/5–74. (Nos. 15237–40 were Diagram 6, and 15254 for some indeterminate reason was given to a 47 ft. bogie brake composite of Diagram 22, which should logically have become 15008.) In 1933 54 still appeared in the list. The breakdown of the renumbering was as follows: –

1933.	1923.	Built.	1933.	1923.	Built.	1933.	1923.	Built.
26653	15187	1893	26670	15208	1893	26688	15251	1896
26654	15188	1893	26671	15211	,,	26689	15255	,,
26655	15189	,,	26672	15212	,,	26690	15256	,,
26656	15193	,,	26673	15213	,,	26691	15257	,,
26657	15194	,,	26674	15215	,,	26692	15268	,,
26658	15195	,,	26675	15216	,,	26693	15269	,,
26659	15196	,,	26676	15217	,,	26694	15270	,,
26660	15197	,,	26677	15218	,,	26695	15272	,,
26661	15198	,, ,,	26678	15225	,,	26696	15273	,,
26662	15199	,,	26679	15227	,,	26697	15274	,,
26663	15200	,,	26680	15228	,,	26698	15262	1897
26664	15201	,,	26681	15229	,,	26699	15263	,,
26665	15202	,,	26682	15231	,,	26700	15264	,,
26666	15204	,,	26683	15232		26701	15243	1898
26667	15205	,,	26684	15241	1894			
26668	15206	,,	26685	15246	1896	27425	15261	1897
26669	15207	,,	26687	15249	,,	27796	15190	1893
						27797	15191	,,
						27798	15224	,,
						27799	15226	,,

27425 had been rebuilt with lavatory, and 27796–9 rebuilt as brake thirds, all at some period between 1923 and 1933, hence the higher numbers than the bulk of the diagram.

The one blank number in the series was probably 15236, and those vehicles scrapped between 1923 and 1933 would be 15192, 15203/9/10/4/9/20/1/2/3/30/3/4/5/42/4/5/50/2/3/8/9/60/5/6/7/71.

Summing all this up, numbers in the 1923 list which cannot be accounted for are 15008, 15076–103, and 15178–86. The solitary six-compartment third of Diagram 7 could possibly have been allotted 15008, and the three remaining Cleminson composites of Diagram 26 could have been 15101–3. This would leave 15076–100 for the four wheeled thirds of Diagram 8, and 15178–86 for the corresponding brake thirds of Diagram 15, (possibly there may have been blanks in both series), but it must be emphasised most explicitly that this is only speculation, and can in no way be proved.

The non-passenger-carrying stock of Diagrams 32–43 were allotted numbers in the 6200's in a separate L.M.S. van series in 1923, altered in 1933 to numbers above 30,000. Very few can be traced, these being as follows: —

Diagram 34.   34' 0" Brake Vans.

1933.	1923.	Built.	1933.	1923.	Built.
34185	6210	1898	34189	6208	1904
34186	6217	,,	34190	6209	,,
34187	6212	1899	34191	6211	,,
34188	6216	,,	34192	6214	1905

Diagram 37.   *21' 0" Horse Box*

43734	6255	1897

Diagram 40.   *18' 0" Open Fish Truck.*

40949	6283	1891

Diagram 43.   *22' 0" Covered Carriage Truck.*

37154	6269	1908

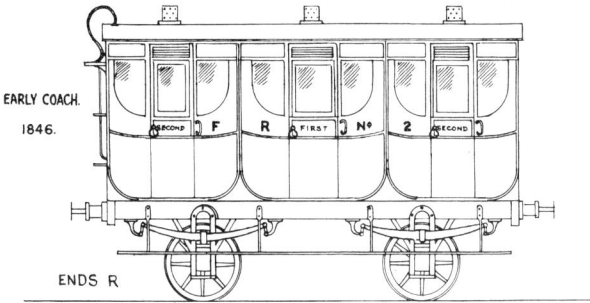

EARLY COACH.

1846.

ENDS R

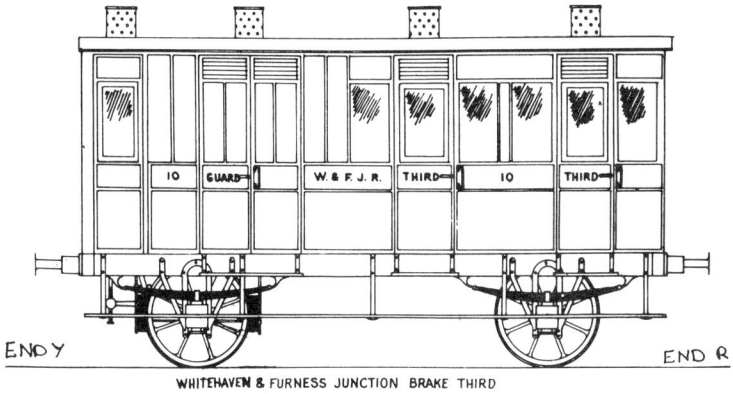

END Y   END R

WHITEHAVEN & FURNESS JUNCTION BRAKE THIRD

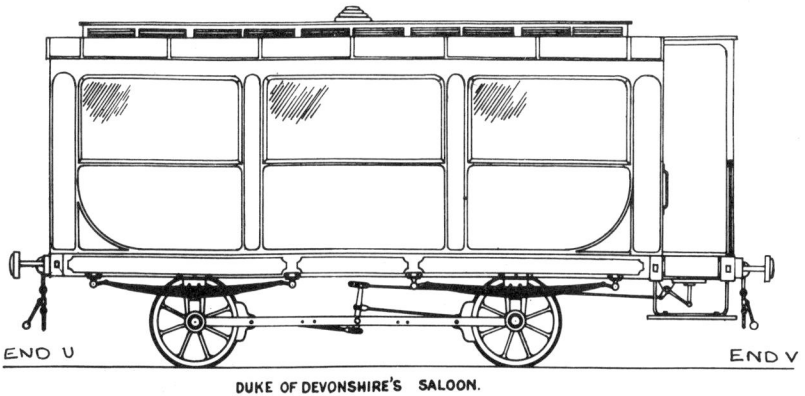

END U   END V

DUKE OF DEVONSHIRE'S SALOON.

35

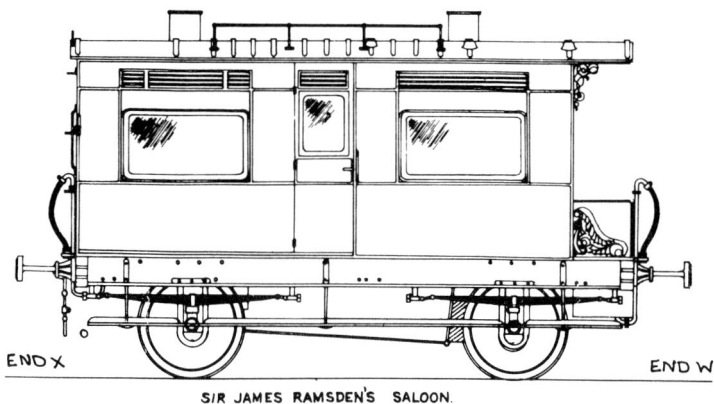

 END X   END W

SIR JAMES RAMSDEN'S SALOON.

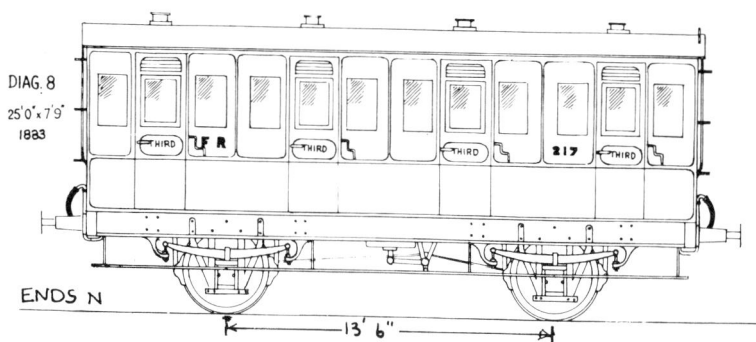

DIAG. 8

25'0" x 7'9"

1883

ENDS N

13' 6"

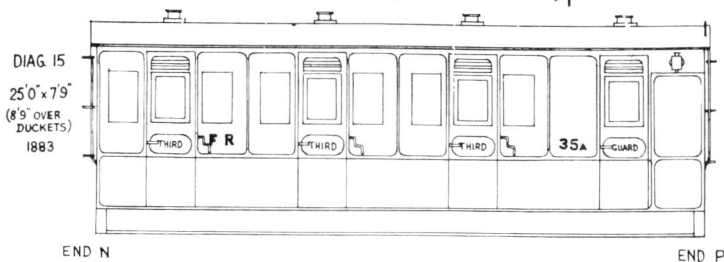

DIAG. 15

25'0" x 7'9"

(8'9" OVER
DUCKETS)

1883

END N   END P

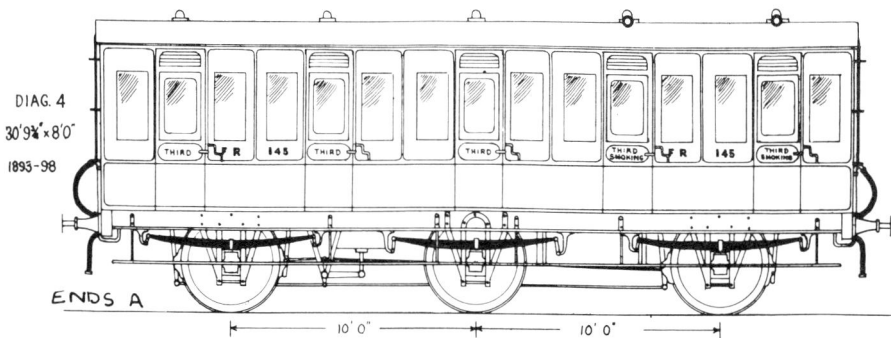

DIAG. 4

30'9¾" x 8'0"

1893-98

ENDS A

10' 0"   10' 0"

36

DIAG. 7
34'3¾" x 8'0"
1884

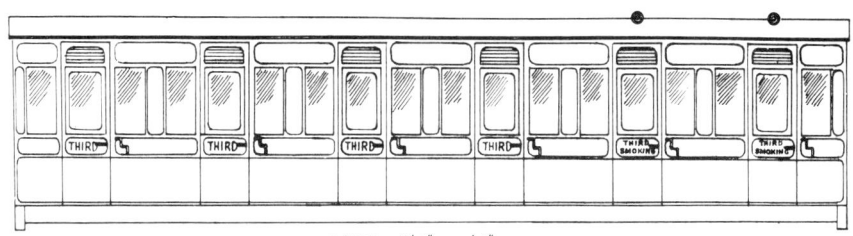

THIRD · THIRD · THIRD · THIRD · THIRD SMOKING · THIRD SMOKING

ENDS A

WHEELBASE   11'0" + 11'0"

DIAG 25
33'9¾" x 8'6"
1890-99

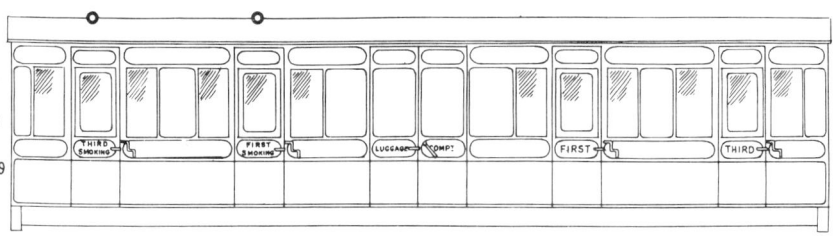

THIRD SMOKING · FIRST SMOKING · LUGGAGE & COMPT · FIRST · THIRD

ENDS A

10'9"   10'9"

PLAN DIAG 20

1ST CLASS

3RD CLASS

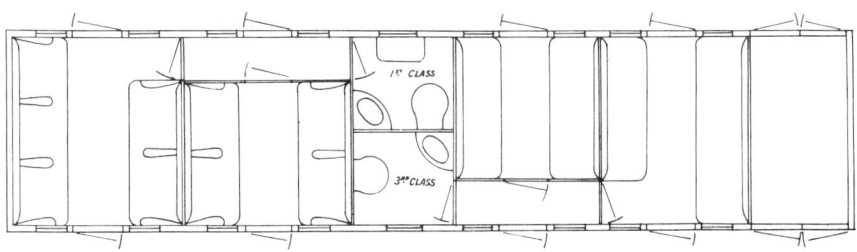

DIAG. 20
35'0" x 8'0"
1900

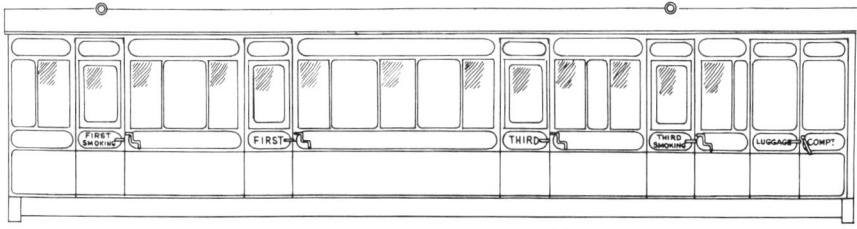

FIRST SMOKING · FIRST · THIRD · THIRD SMOKING · LUGGAGE & COMPT

ENDS C.

11'0"   11'0"

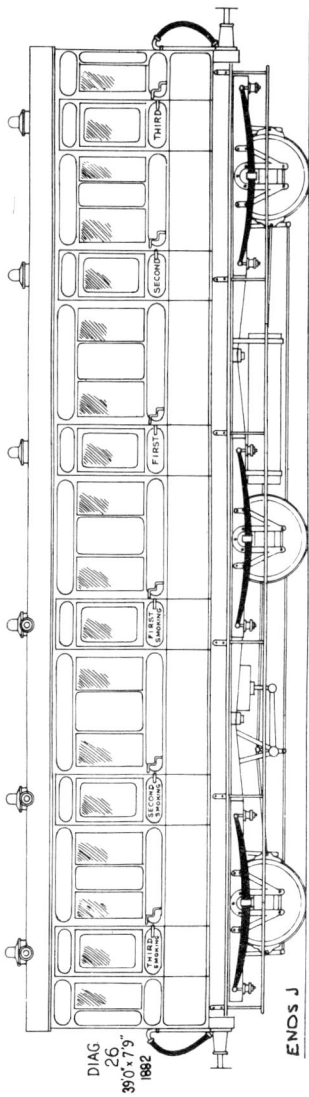

DIAG. 26
39'0" x 7'9"
1882

ENDS J

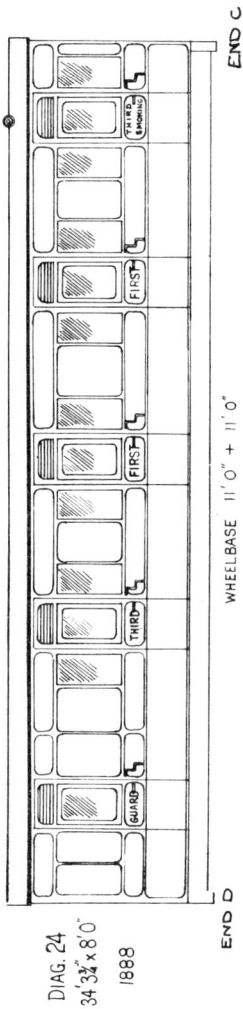

DIAG. 24
34'3¾" x 8'0"
1888

END C

WHEELBASE 11'0" + 11'0"

END D

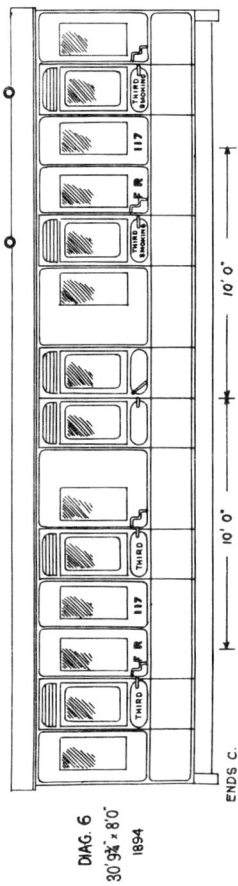

DIAG. 6
30'9¾" x 8'0"
1894

10'0"

10'0"

ENDS C.

38

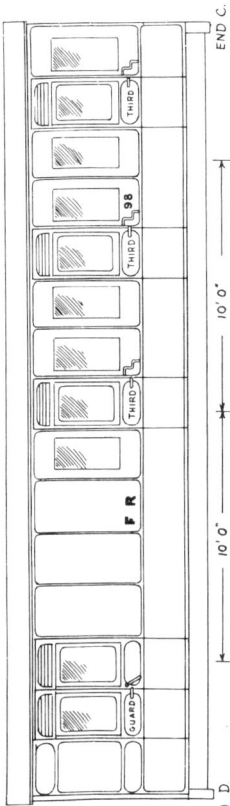

DIAG. 14
30'9¾" x 8'0"
(8'10" OVER
DUCKETS)
1894-95

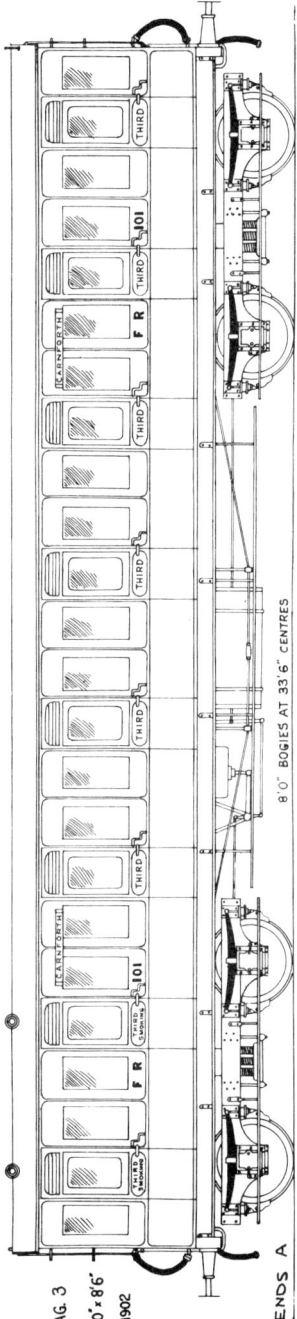

END C.

END D

THIRD

98

THIRD

THIRD

F R

GUARD

10'0"

10'0"

10'0"

DIAG. 3
48'0" x 8'6"
1902

ENDS A

THIRD

101

THIRD

CARNFORTH

F R

THIRD

THIRD

THIRD
SMOKING

CARNFORTH

F R

101

THIRD

THIRD
SMOKING

8'0" BOGIES AT 33'6" CENTRES

NOTE - DIAG. 2 WAS EXACTLY SIMILAR TO DIAG. 3, BUT 49'0" LONG.

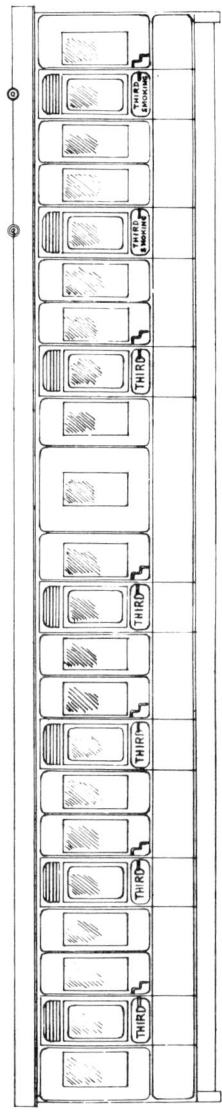

DIAG. 10
43'6" x 8'0"
1903-1907

ENDS H

THIRD
SMOKING

THIRD
SMOKING

THIRD

THIRD

THIRD

THIRD

THIRD
SMOKING

8'0" BOGIES AT 28'6" CENTRES

39

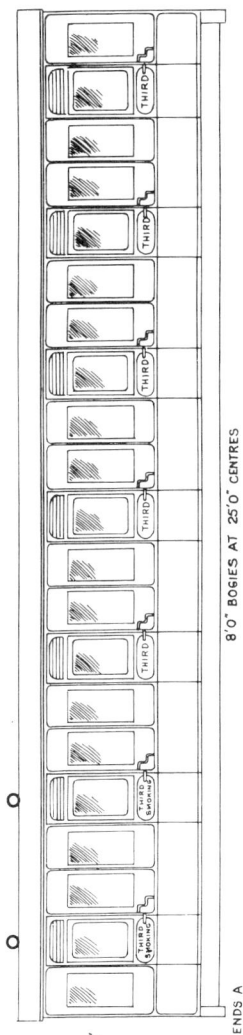

DIAG. 4A
40'0" × 8'6"
1902-03

8'0" BOGIES AT 25'0" CENTRES

ENDS A

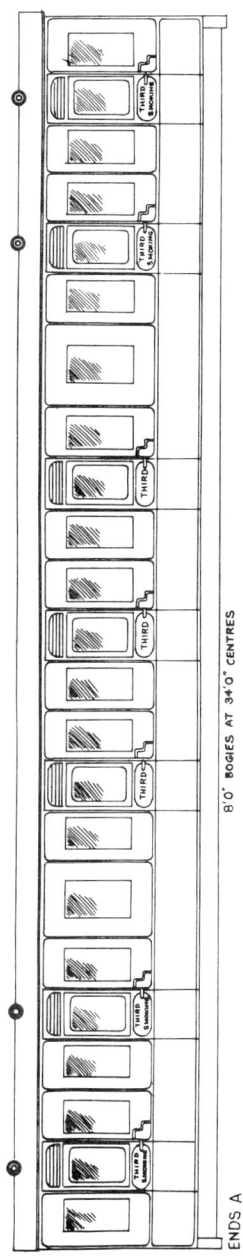

DIAG 9
40'0" × 8'6"
1904

8'0" BOGIES AT 34'0" CENTRES

ENDS A

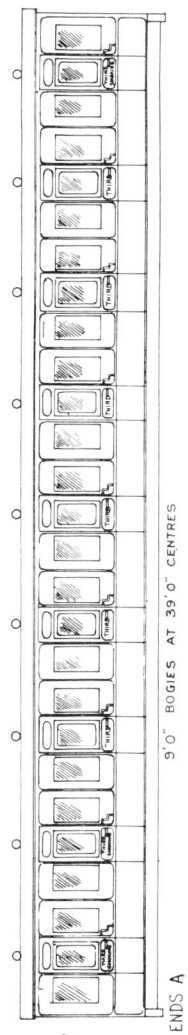

DIAG. 1
57'0" × 9'0"
1919-1921

9'0" BOGIES AT 39'0" CENTRES

ENDS A

40

8'0" BOGIES AT 34'0" CENTRES.

ENDS A

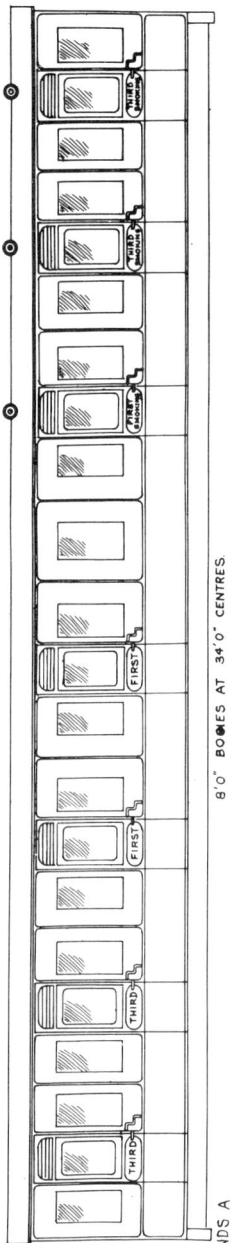

DIAG.
19
49'0" x 8'6"
1903

8'0" BOGIES AT 33'0' CENTRES

END A

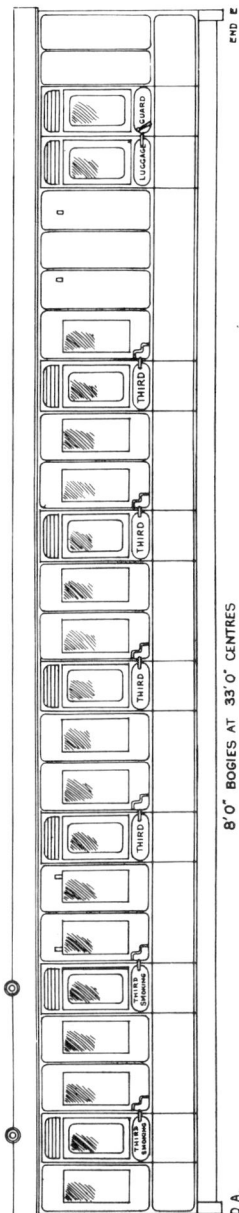

DIAG.13
48'0" x 8'6"
1901-02

8'0" BOGIES AT 34'0' CENTRES

END A

END E

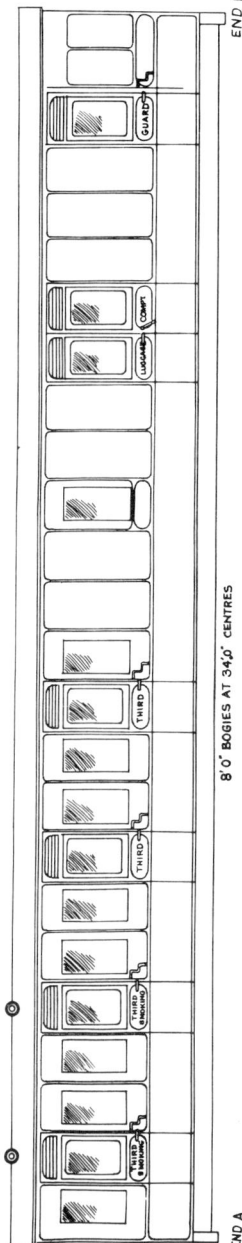

DIAG.
11
49'0" x
8'6"
(9'0 OVER
ENDSTEPS)
1908-15

41

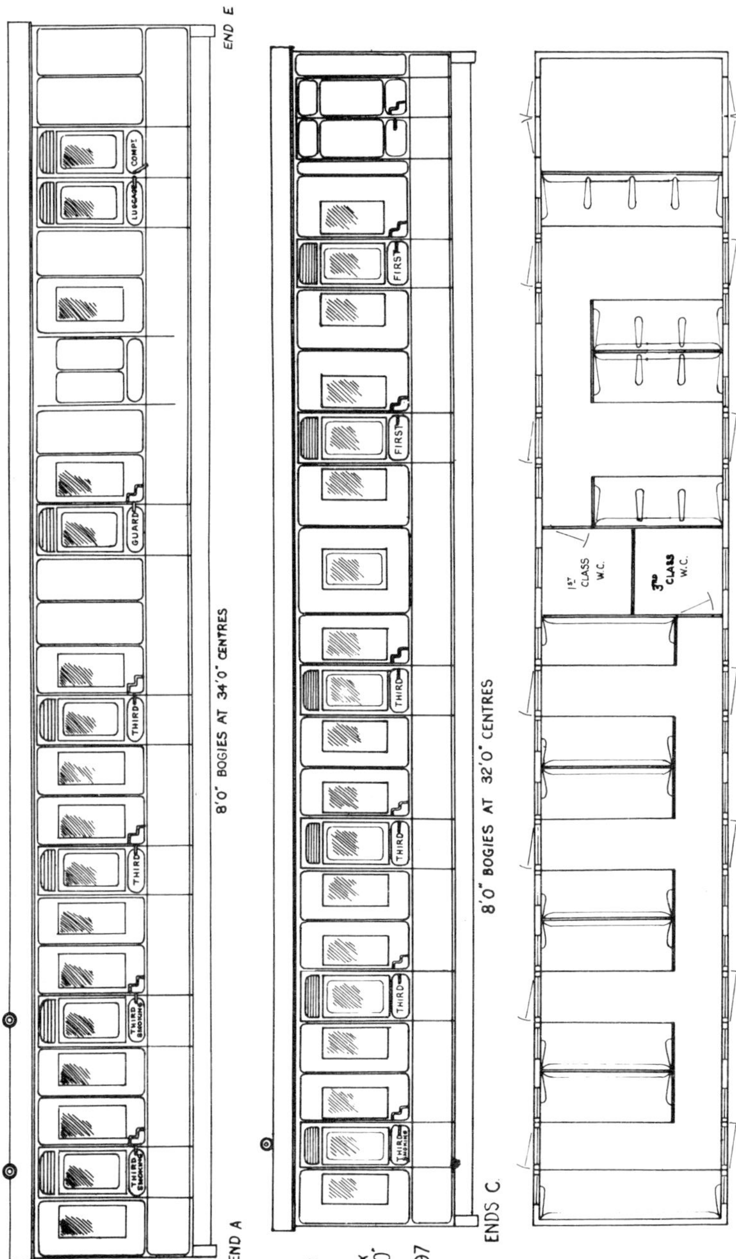

END E

END A

8'0" BOGIES AT 34'0" CENTRES

DIAG.
12
49'0" x
8'6"
(9'0" OVER
DROIPS)
1906-07

GUARD

LUGGAGE COMPT.

THIRD

THIRD

THIRD
SMOKING

THIRD
SMOKING

ENDS C

8'0" BOGIES AT 32'0" CENTRES

DIAG
21
47'0" x
8'0"
1897

FIRST

FIRST

THIRD

THIRD

THIRD

THIRD

1ST
CLASS
W.C.

3RD
CLASS
W.C.

42

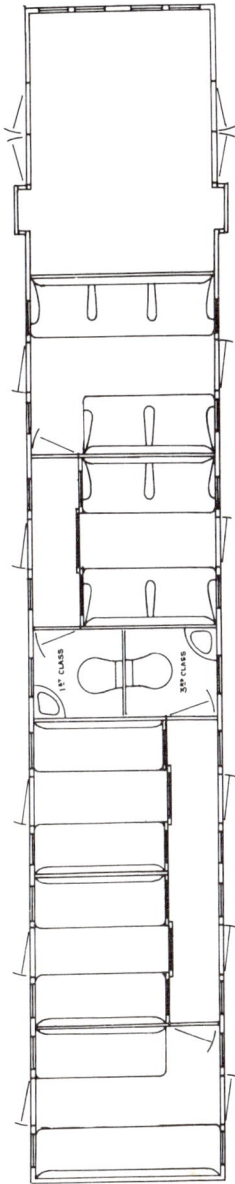

PLAN.
DIAG 22

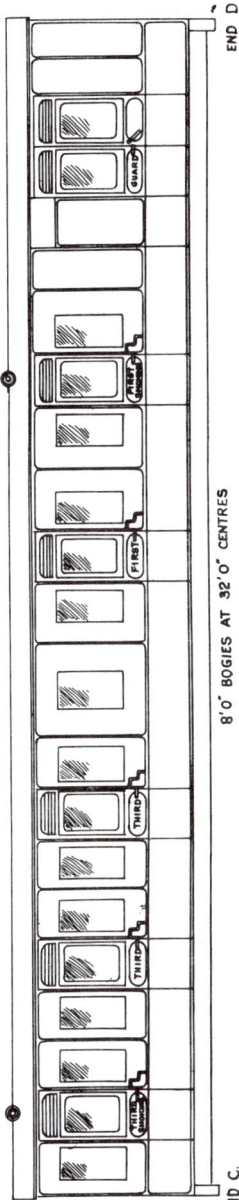

DIAG.
22
47'0" x 8'0"
(8'10" OVER
DUCKETS)
1897

END C.

END D

8'0" BOGIES AT 32'0" CENTRES

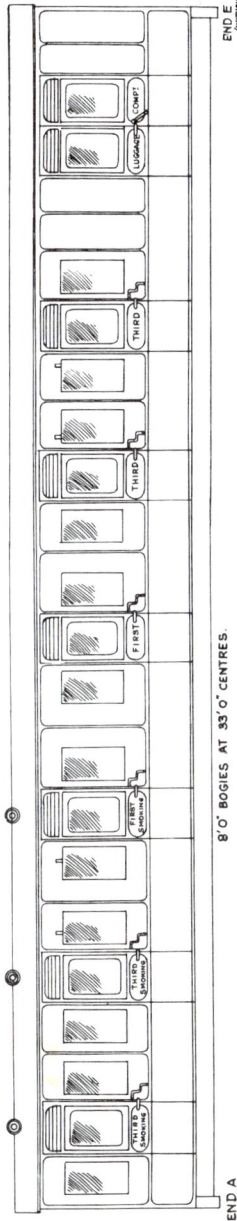

DIAG. 23
48'0" x 8'6"
1902

END A

END E
(WITHOUT DUCKETS)

8'0" BOGIES AT 33'0" CENTRES.

GUARD

FIRST SMOKING

FIRST

THIRD

THIRD

THIRD SMOKING

LUGGAGE COMP?

THIRD

FIRST

FIRST SMOKING

THIRD SMOKING

THIRD SMOKING

1? CLASS

3?? CLASS

43

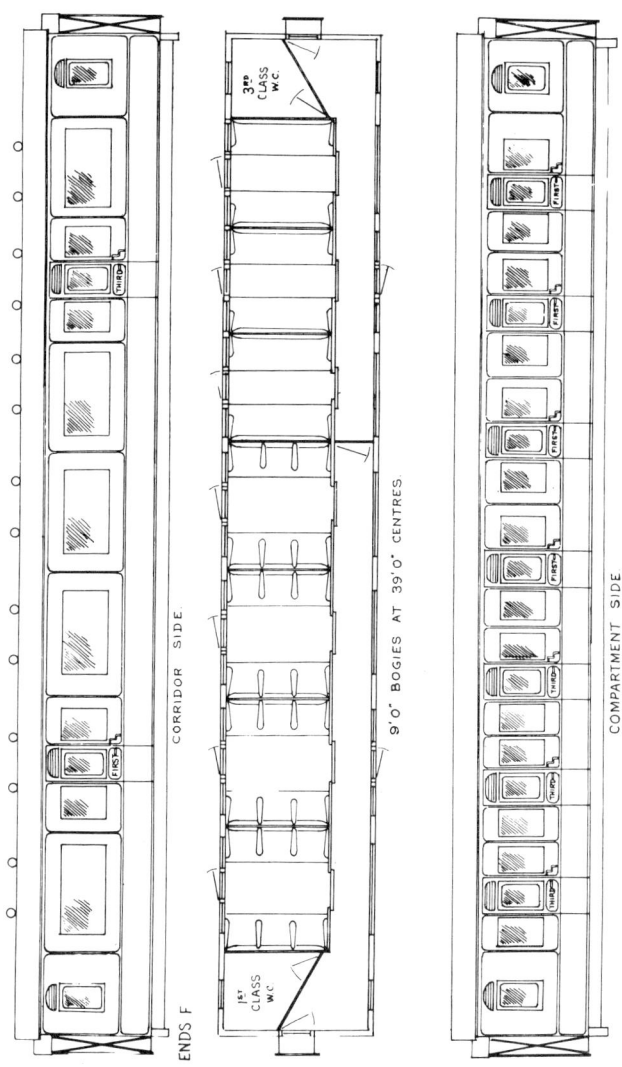

CORRIDOR SIDE

ENDS F

3RD CLASS W.C.

1ST CLASS W.C.

9'0" BOGIES AT 39'0" CENTRES

DIAG. 17

57'0" x 9'0"

1921-1924

COMPARTMENT SIDE

DIAG. 16   49'0" × 8'6"   1904-1914

COMPARTMENT SIDE

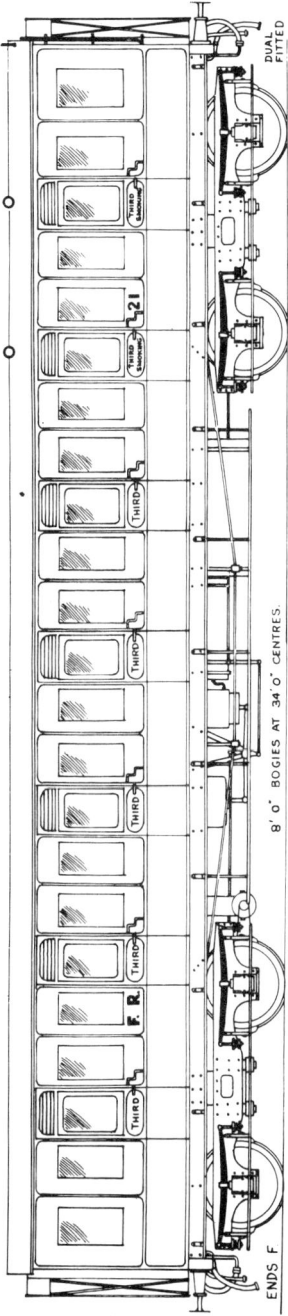

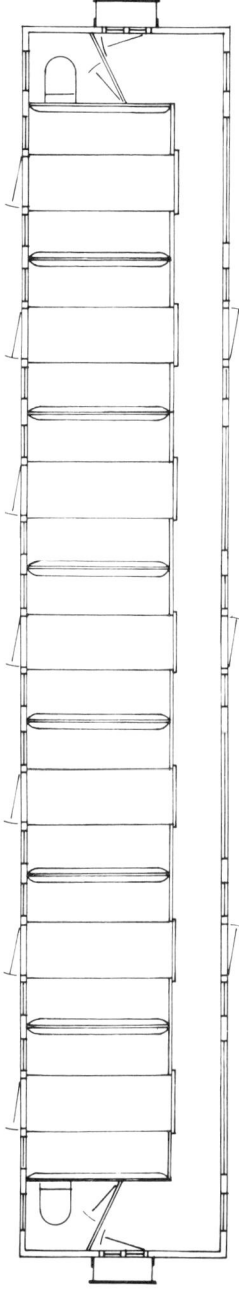

THIRD   21   THIRD   THIRD   THIRD   THIRD   F.R.   THIRD

DUAL FITTED

8' 0' BOGIES AT 34'0' CENTRES

ENDS F

CORRIDOR SIDE

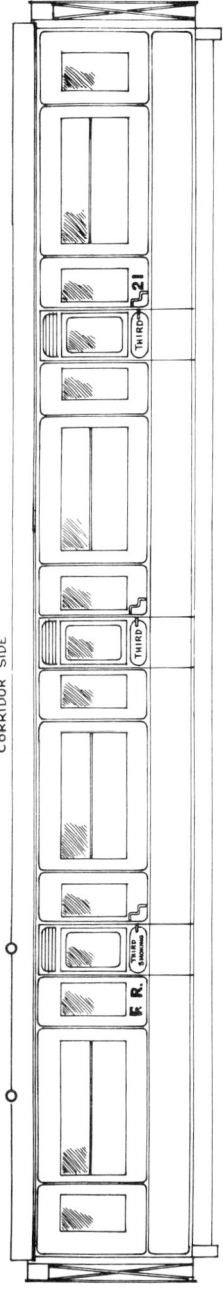

THIRD   21   THIRD   THIRD   F.R.

45

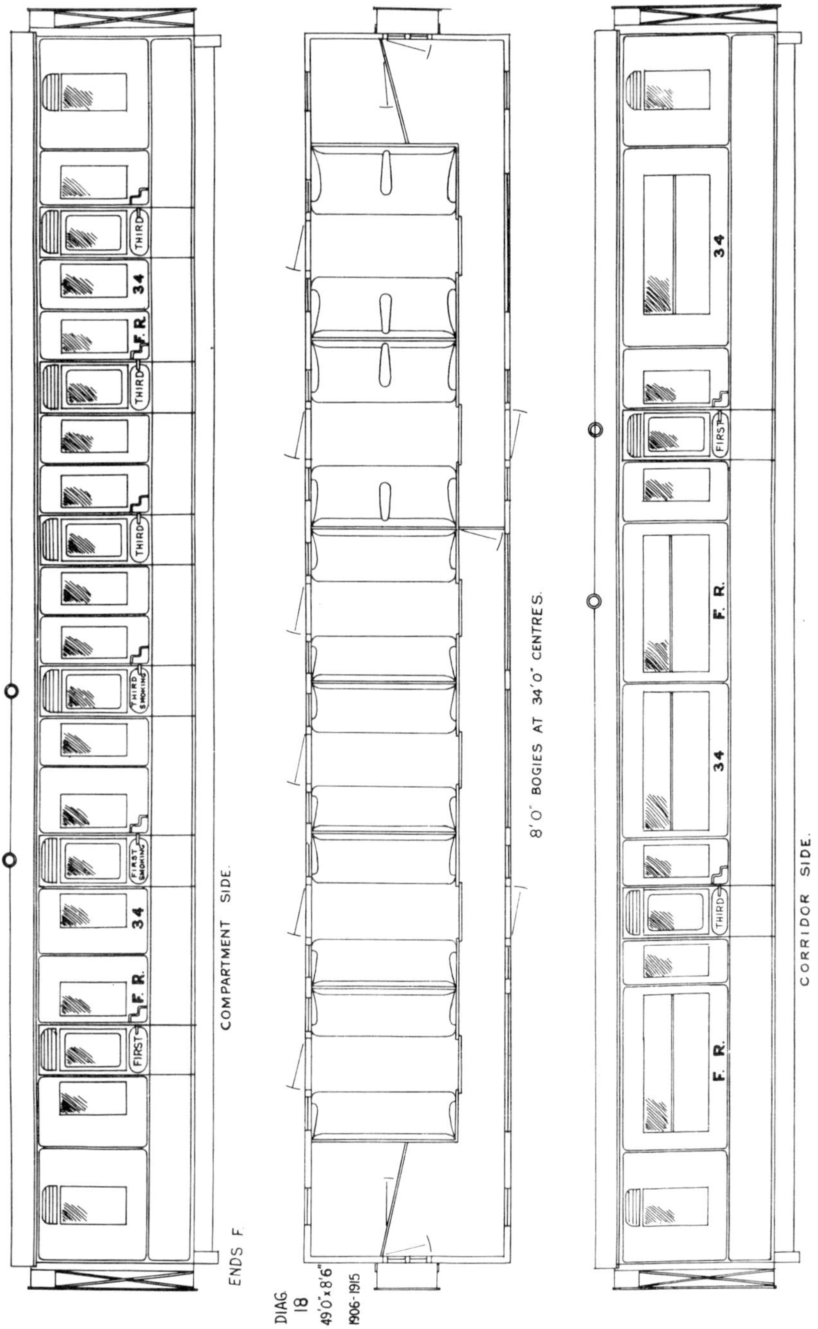

THIRD 34 F.R. THIRD THIRD THIRD SMOKING FIRST SMOKING 34 F.R. FIRST

COMPARTMENT SIDE.

ENDS F

DIAG.
18
49'0"x8'6"
1906-1915

8'0" BOGIES AT 34'0" CENTRES.

34 FIRST F.R. 34 THIRD F.R.

CORRIDOR SIDE.

46

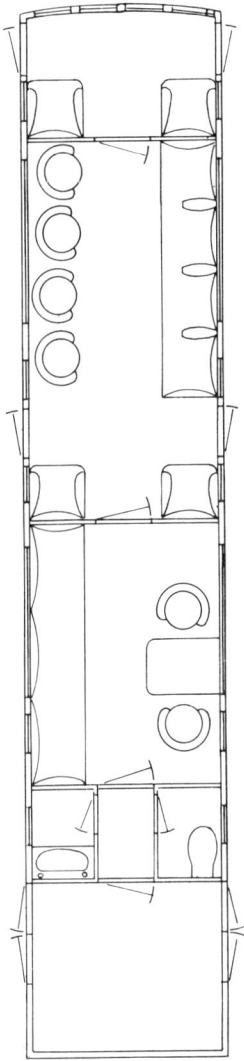

PLAN.
DIAG. 28

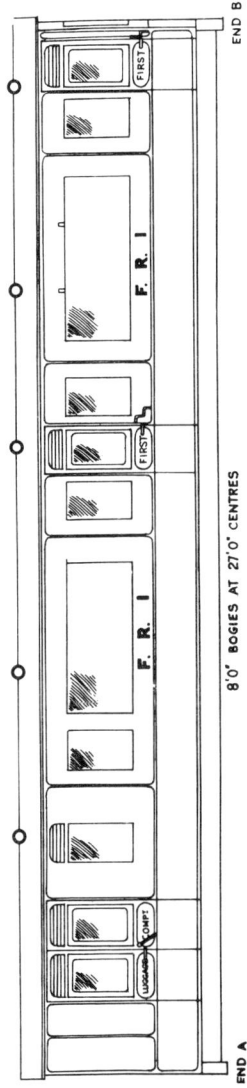

DIAG. 28
42'0" x 8'4"
1899

FIRST

F. R. I

FIRST

F. R. I

LUGGAGE & COMPT.

END B

END A

8'0" BOGIES AT 27'0" CENTRES

47

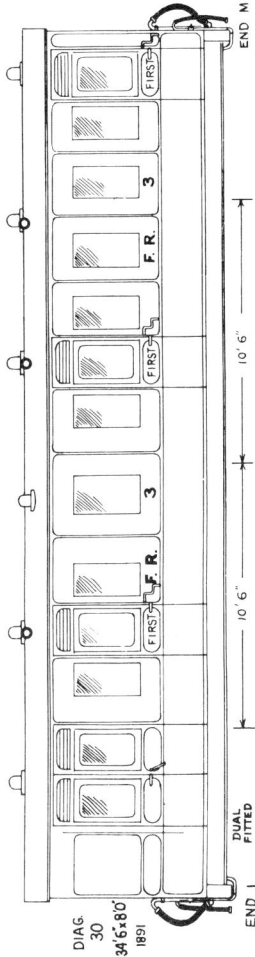

DIAG. 30
34'6"×8'0"
1891

DUAL FITTED

END L

END M

10'6"

10'6"

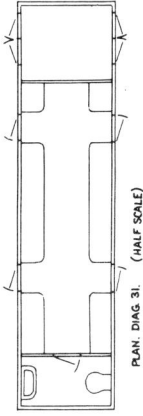

PLAN. DIAG 31. (HALF SCALE)

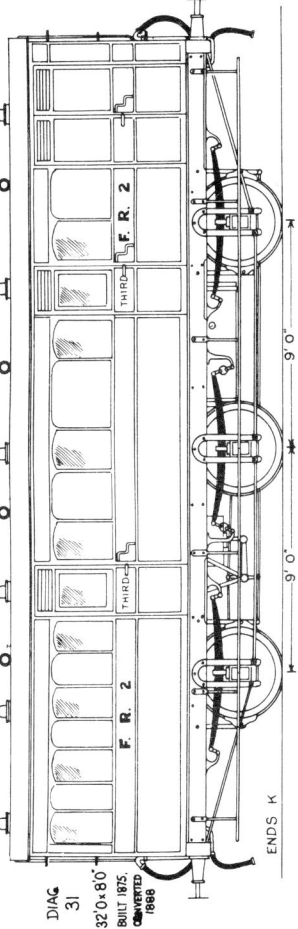

DIAG 31
32'0"×8'0"
BUILT 1875.
CONVERTED 1888

ENDS K

9'0"

9'0"

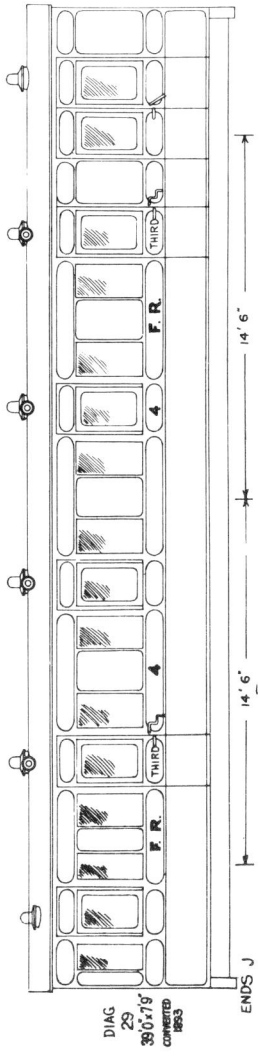

DIAG 29
39'0"×7'9"
CONVERTED 1893

ENDS J

14'6"

14'6"

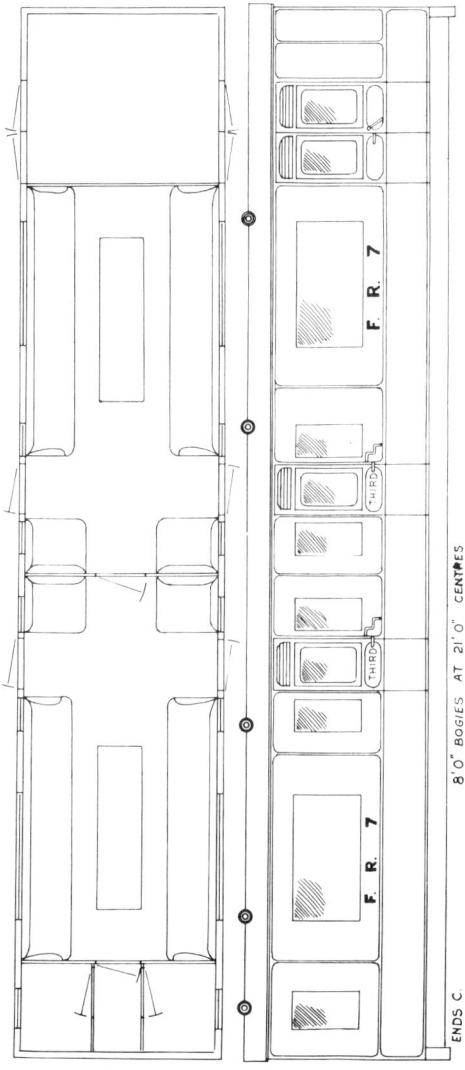

PLAN
DIAG 27

DIAG.
27
42'0" x 8'6"
1900

F. R. 7

THIRD

THIRD

F. R. 7

8'0" BOGIES AT 21'0" CENTRES

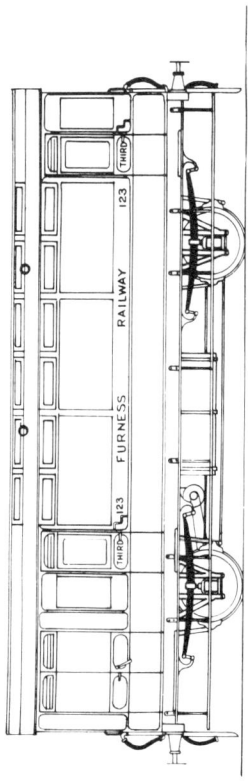

ENDS C.

THIRD   123

FURNESS   RAILWAY

123   THIRD

ENDS T

rail motor trailer

49

DIAG. 33   MAIL VAN Nº 1   1887   WHEELBASE 14'0"
22'6" × 8'0"

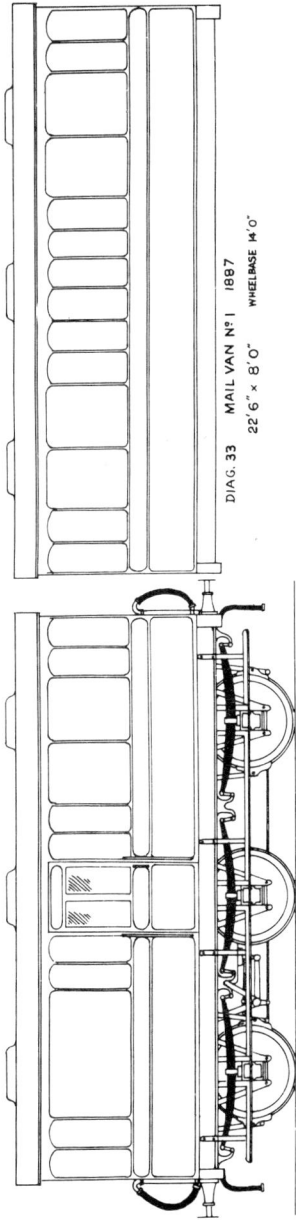

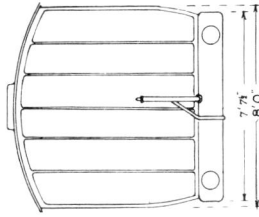

DIAG. 32   MAIL VAN Nº 2   1903   WHEELBASE 21'0"
32'0" × 8'0"

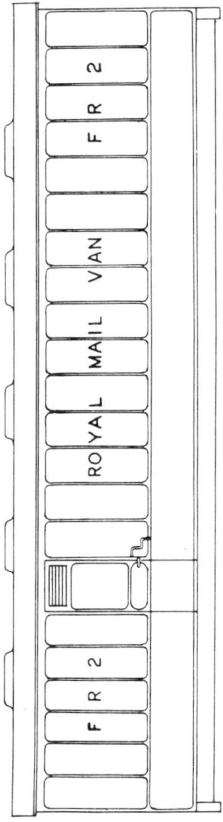

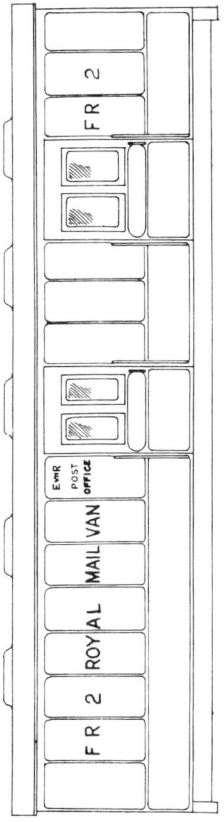

7'7¼"
8'0"

F R 2

ROYAL MAIL VAN

F R 2

F R 2

E^mR
POST
OFFICE

F R 2   ROYAL MAIL VAN

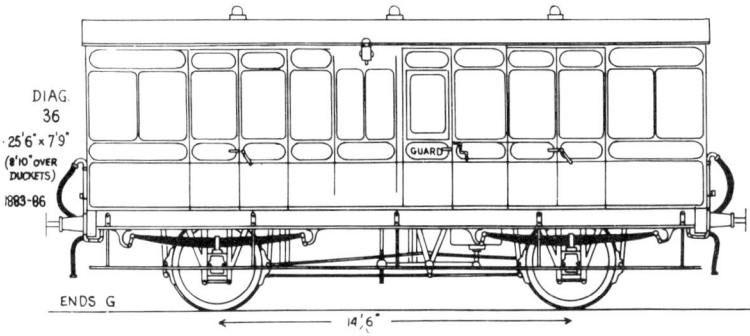

DIAG.
36
25'6" x 7'9"
(8'10" OVER
DUCKETS)
1883-86

GUARD

ENDS G

14'6"

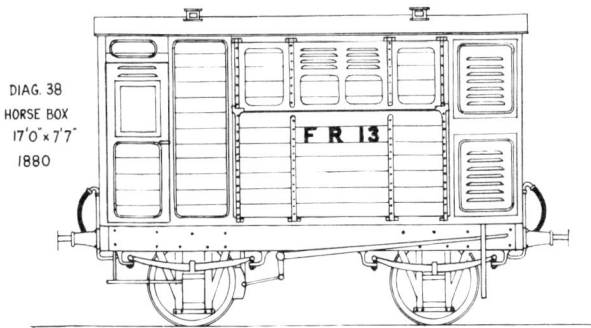

DIAG. 38
HORSE BOX
17'0" x 7'7"
1880

F R 13

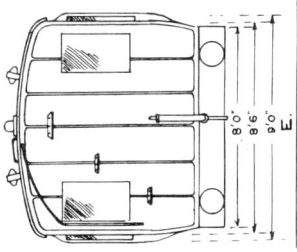

E.

8'0"
8'6"
9'0"

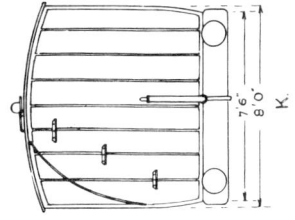

K.

7'6"
8'0"

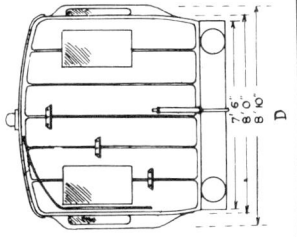

D.

7'6"
8'0"
8'6"

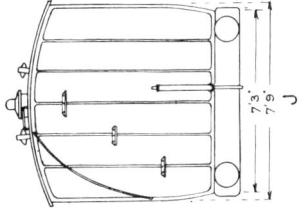

J.

7'3"
7'9"

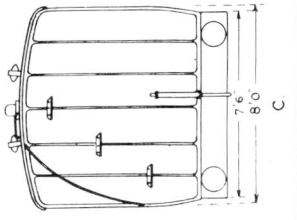

C.

7'6"
8'0"

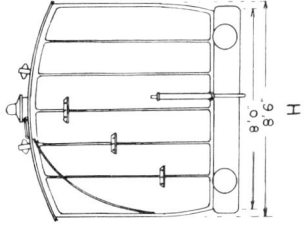

H.

8'0"
8'6"

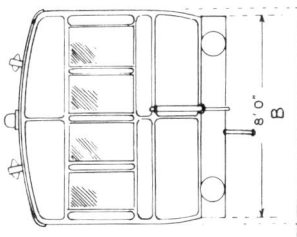

B.

8'0"
8'6"

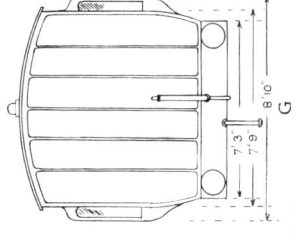

G.

7'3"
7'9"
8'10"

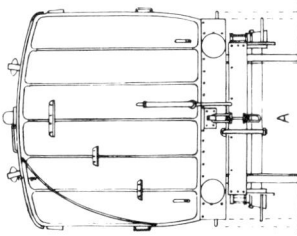

A.

8'0"
8'6"

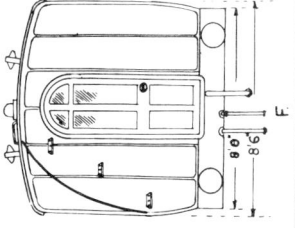

F.

8'0"
8'6"

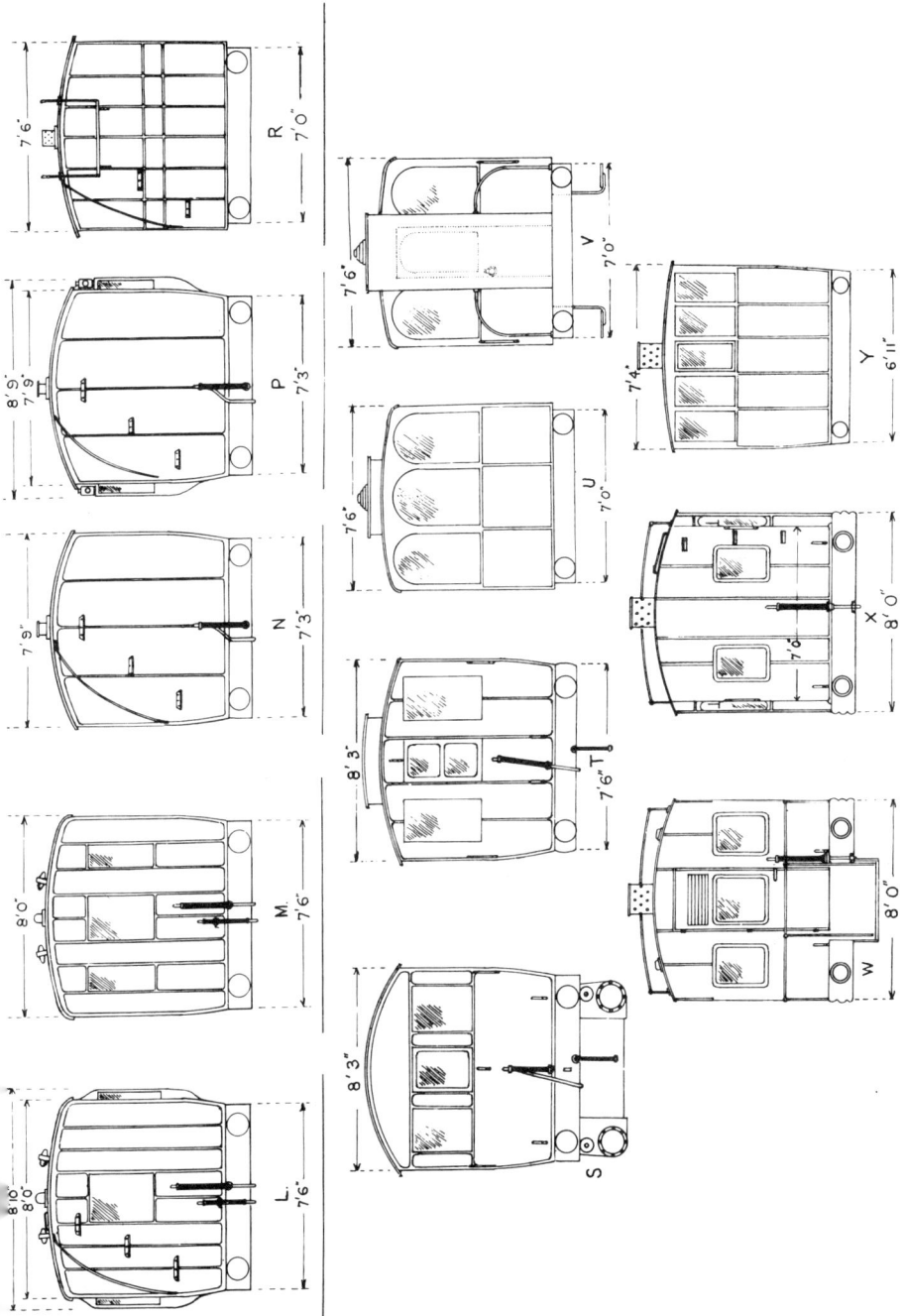

R
7'6"
7'0"

P
8'9"
7'9"
7'3"

N
7'9"
7'3"

M
8'0"
7'6"

L
8'10"
8'0"
7'6"

V
7'6"
7'0"

U
7'6"
7'0"

T
8'3"
7'6"

S
8'3"

Y
7'4"
6'11"

X
7'6"
8'0"

W
8'0"

GOODS STOCK

F.R. Diag.	Type	Tons.	Planks.	Wheels.	Dimensions.	Date.	No. Built.	F.R. Nos. (Where Known)
1.	Open Wagon	6	1	4	15' 0" x 7' 3½"	1880	103	
2.	,,	10	2	4	17' 5" x 7' 5"	1880+	695	
3.	,,	10	2	4	15' 0" x 7' 3½"	1884–90	1356	
4.	,,	10	2	4	15' 0" x 7' 6"	1899	100	7178–277
5.	,,	8	2	4	15' 0" x 7' 4"	1890	30	
6.	,,	15	3	4	17'11" x 7'11"	1906	10	
7.	,,	10*	3	4	16' 0" x 7'10"	1909+	839	7623–32
8.	,,	12	3	4	16' 0" x 7'10"	1909	17	4746–77
9.	,,	10	4	4	16' 0" x 7'10"	1914–19	382	2201–17
10.	,,	10	3	4	15' 0" x 7' 4"	1878+	220	2549
11.	,,	10	4	4	15' 0" x 7' 4"	1880+	225	
12.	,,	10*	3	4	17' 5" x 7' 5"	1880	30	4057–60
13.	,,	10	4	4	16' 0" x 7' 6"	1900	158	7320–477
14.	,,	10*	4	4	16' 7" x 7' 6"	1900	50	7278–319
15.	,,	10	5	4	16' 0" x 7' 6"	1909	73	
16.	,,	12	5	4	16' 0" x 7'10"	1914–19	31	
17.	,,	15*	4	4	18' 0" x 7'10"	1906	90	7633–722
18.	Van	10*	10	4	16' 0" x 8' 4"	1906	10	7598–607
19.	,,	10*	9	4	16' 0" x 8' 0½"	1903	10	7588–97
20.	,,	10*	10	4	16' 0" x 8' 0½"	1906	15	7608–22
21.	,,	10	10	4	14' 0" x 7' 8"	1907	45	6417–61
22.	,,	10	10	4	16' 1" x 7' 8"	1907–13	208	
23.	,,	10		8	?	1884	?	
24.	Ore Wagon	45	6	8	?	1914	?	
25.	Coke Wagon	10	5+2	4	16' 6" x 7' 6"	1880	535	614
26.	Ore Wagon	10	7	4	15' 0" x 6' 8½"	1887+	319	2772
27.	,,	10	5	4	14'11" x 7' 3½"	1897+	35	6859–7177
28.	,,	10	4	4	15' 0" x 7' 4"	1898	50	308–42
29.	,,	10	4	4	15' 0" x 7' 6"	1900	25	7484–533
30.	Steel Hopper	12*	—	4	12' 0" x 4' 1½"	1907	26	7723–47
31.	,,	12*	—	4	12' 0" x 5' 0"	1912	38	7797–822
32.	,,	12	—	4	12' 0" x 5' 6"	1915		7843–80

No.	Type			Dimensions	Date	Total	F.R. Numbers
33.	Ore Wagon	20*	8	16' 0" x 7' 6"	1903	25	258–82
34.	,,	12	6	15' 0" x 7' 6"	1906+	187	71–257
35.	,,	20	8	16' 0" x 7' 5"	1903	25	283–307
36.	Coke Wagon	10*	10	20' 0" x 7' 5"	1905	43	515–57
37.	Loco. Coal	12	10	18' 6" x 7' 6"	1905	17	558–74
38.	,,	15*	7	17' 0" x 7' 10"	1913	20	7748–67
39.	,,	10*	7	18' 0" x 7' 10"	1907	19	
40.	Explosives	10*	—	14' 1" x 7' 7"	1913	6	2559–62, 5666/7.
41.	Well Wagon	35*	—	44' 0" x 8' 1"	1902	1	7536
42.	Timber Truck	10	1	15' 0" x 7' 3½"	1883+	24	
43.	Bolster	12	1	13' 6" x 6' 8"	1889–1919	585	7478–83
44.	Rail Wagon	15	—	31' 0" x 7' 7"	1913	20	7823–42
45.	,,	25*	—	25' 6" x 6' 7"	1903	50	7538–87
46.	Bolster	10*	—	34' 0" x 8' 0"	1918	6	
47.	Wood Pulp	8	7	23' 0" x 7' 0"	1906	25	1516–40
48.	Cattle Truck	8	7	13' 6" x 8' 0"	1890	27	
49.	,,	10	7	15' 6" x 8' 0"	1882	6	2822–9
50.	,,	10	7	15' 6" x 8' 0"	1906	62	
51.	,,			18' 0" x 8' 0"	1906	38	
52.	,, ?						
52A.	Brake Van	12	11	16' 0" x 7' 7"	1917	3	35, 41, 50
53.	,,	10	11	16' 0" x 7' 7"	1907	27	61–87
54.	,,	10	11	15' 0" x 7' 5½"	1880+	57	13A, 47, 24–33
55.	Ballast Truck	6	2	15' 0" x 7' 3½"	1884–99	60	

F.R. numbering is taken from the Diagram Book, and in many cases is incomplete. + after a building date denotes that these wagons were built over a period not stated, the date given being that of the first batch. Diagram 49 Cattle trucks were roofless.

*Steel underframes

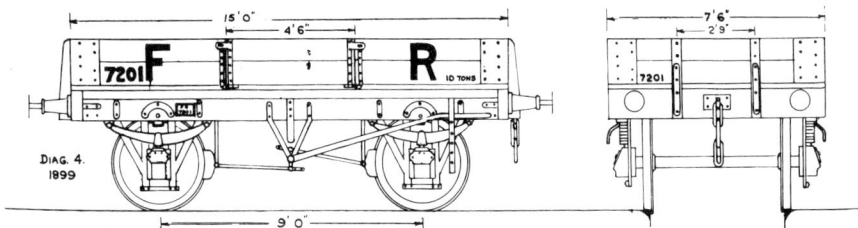

DIAG. 4.
1899

15' 0"
4' 6"
7' 6"
2' 9"
9' 0"

F R
7201
7201
10 TONS

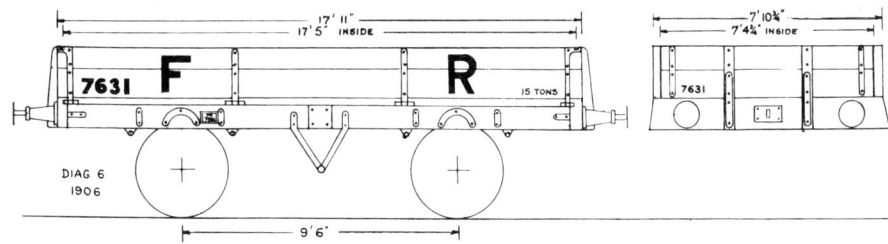

DIAG 6
1906

17' 11"
17' 5" INSIDE
7' 10¾"
7' 4¾" INSIDE
9' 6"

F R
7631
7631
15 TONS

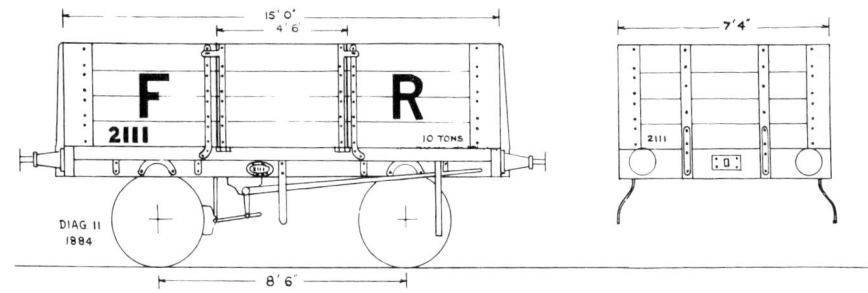

DIAG 11
1884

15' 0"
4' 6"
7' 4"
8' 6"

F R
2111
2111
10 TONS

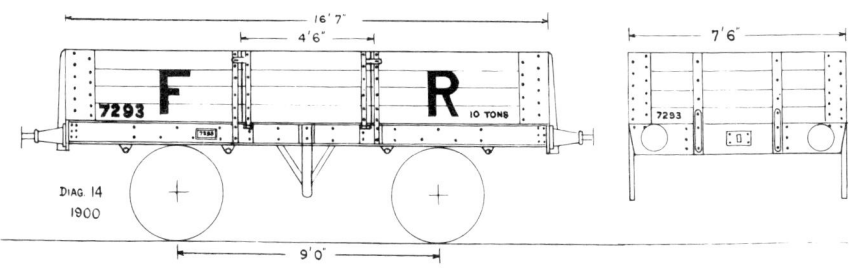

DIAG. 14
1900

16' 7"
4' 6"
7' 6"
9' 0"

F R
7293
7293
10 TONS

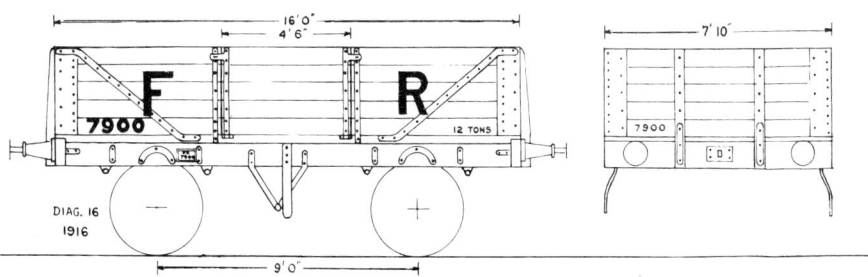

DIAG. 16
1916

16' 0"
4' 6"
7' 10"
9' 0"

F R
7900
7900
12 TONS

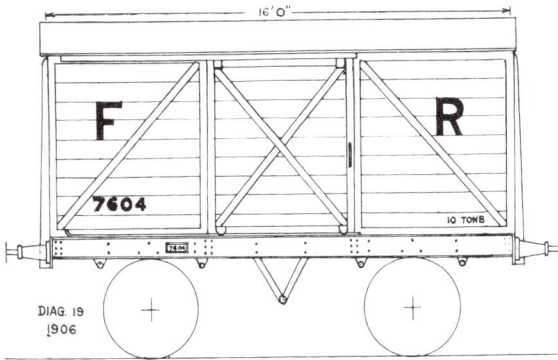

F R
7604
10 TONS

DIAG. 19
1906

16' 0"
9' 0"

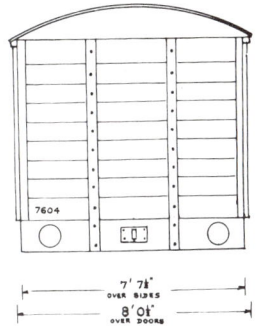

7604

7' 7½"
OVER SIDES
8' 0½"
OVER DOORS

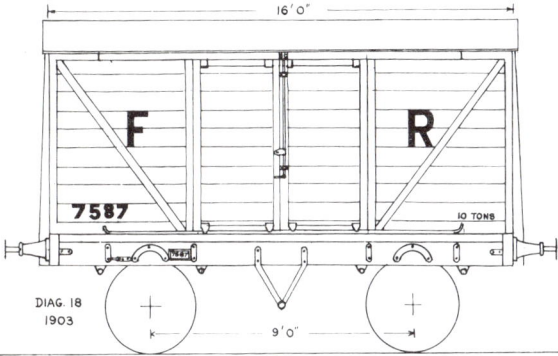

F R
7587
10 TONS

DIAG. 18
1903

16' 0"
9' 0"

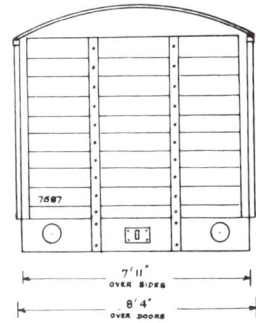

7587

7' 11"
OVER SIDES
8' 4"
OVER DOORS

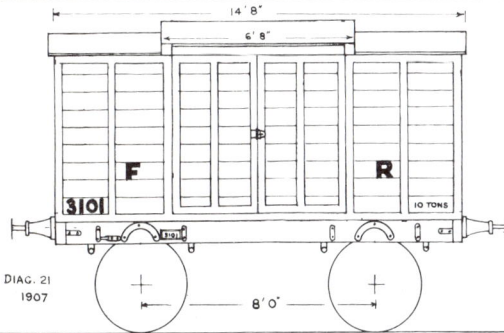

F R
3101
10 TONS

DIAG. 21
1907

14' 8"
6' 8"
8' 0"

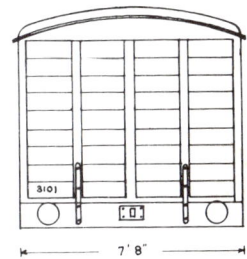

3101

7' 8"

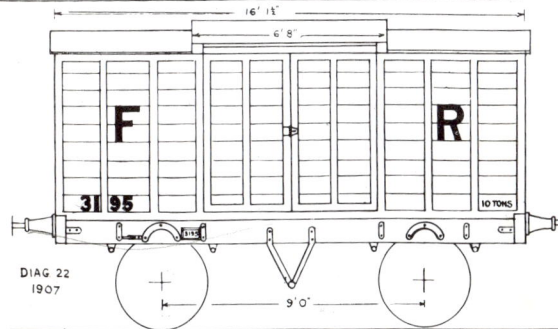

F R
31 95
10 TONS

DIAG 22
1907

16' 1½"
6' 8"
9' 0"

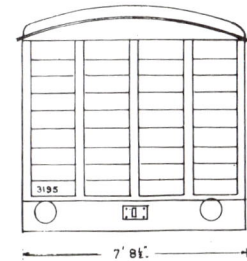

3195

7' 8½"

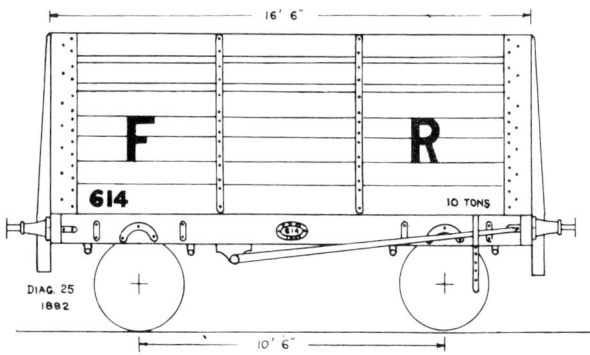

16' 6"
7' 6"
3' 0"

F R
614
10 TONS

DIAG. 25
1882
10' 6"

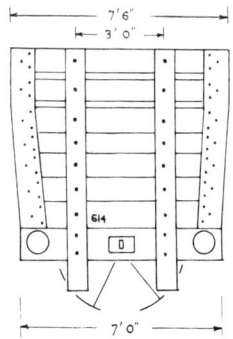

614
7' 0"

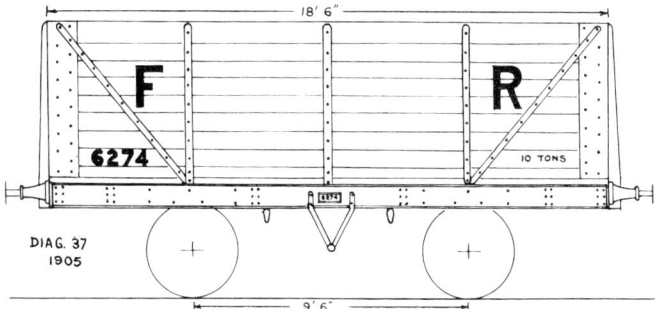

18' 6"

F R
6274
10 TONS

DIAG. 37
1905
9' 6"

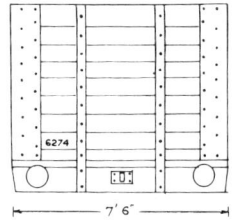

7' 6"
6274

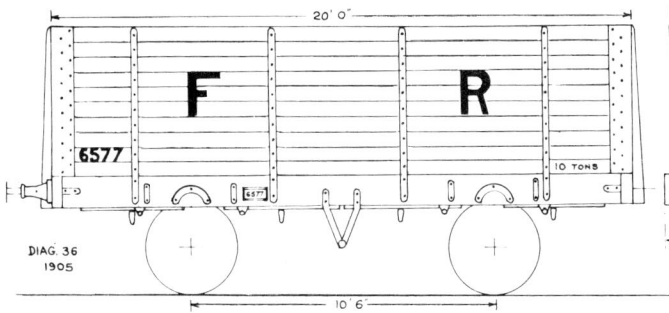

20' 0"

F R
6577
10 TONS

DIAG. 36
1905
10' 6"

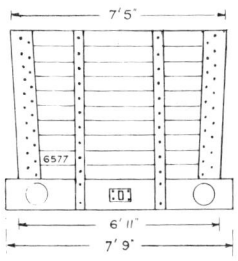

7' 5"
6577
6' 11"
7' 9"

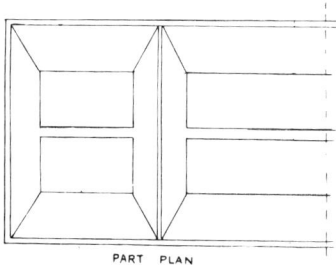

PART PLAN

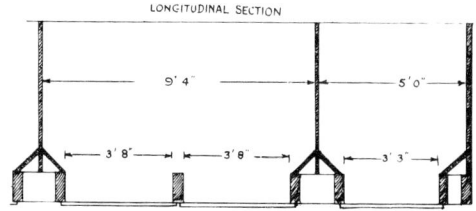

LONGITUDINAL SECTION

9' 4"   5' 0"
3' 8"   3' 8"   3' 3"

DIAG. 36

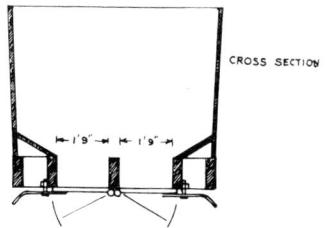

CROSS SECTION

1' 9" 1' 9"

15' 0"

3' 6"

F   R

2772

2772

DIAG. 26
1887

9' 0"

6' 8"

6' 0"

DIAG. 26.

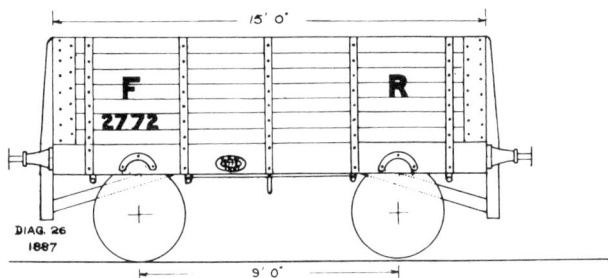

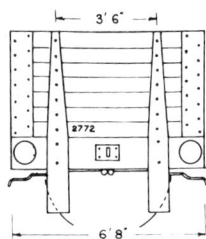

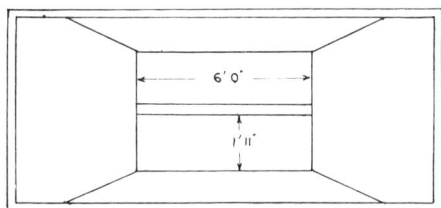

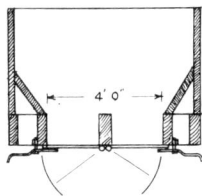

PLAN & SECTION
OF HOPPER.

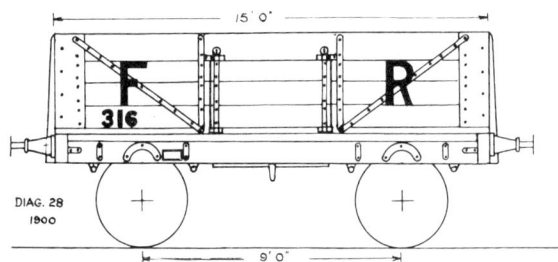

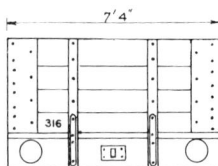

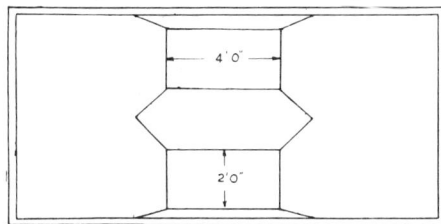

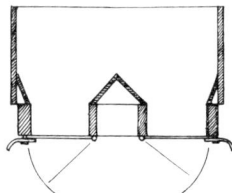

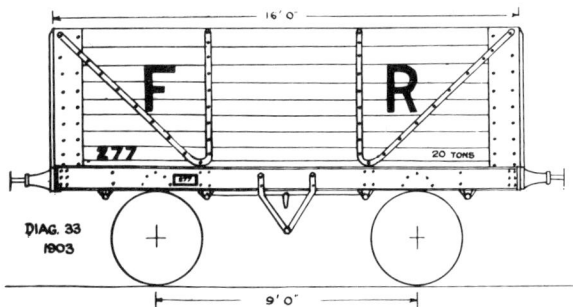

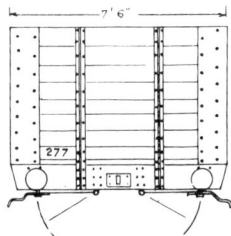

4' 0"

1' 11"

15' 0"

7' 4"

F   R

316

316

DIAG. 28
1900

9' 0"

4' 0"

DIAG. 28.

PLAN & SECTION
OF HOPPER.

2' 0"

16' 0"

7' 6"

F   R

277

20 TONS

277

DIAG. 33
1903

9' 0"

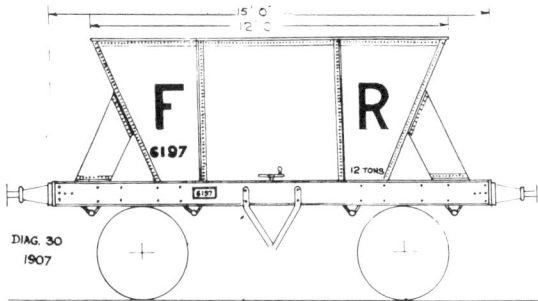
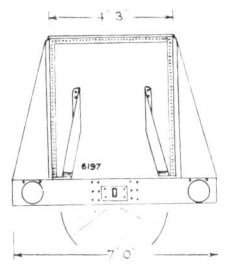

F **R**
6197   12 TONS

DIAG. 30
1907

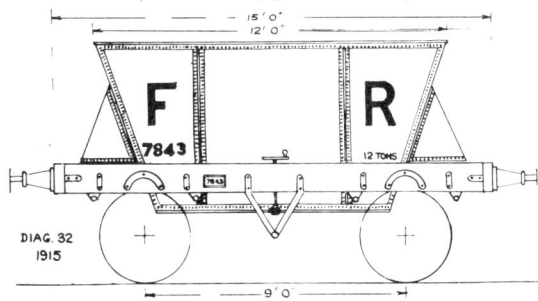
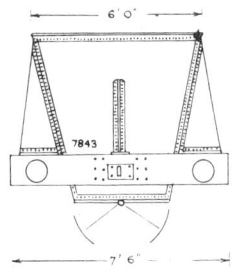

F **R**
7843   12 TONS

DIAG. 32
1915

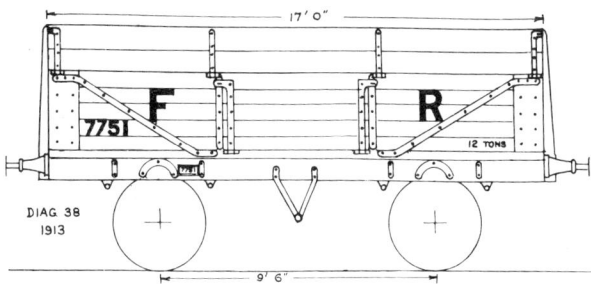
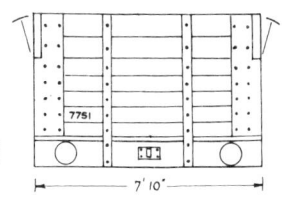

F **R**
7751   12 TONS

DIAG. 38
1913

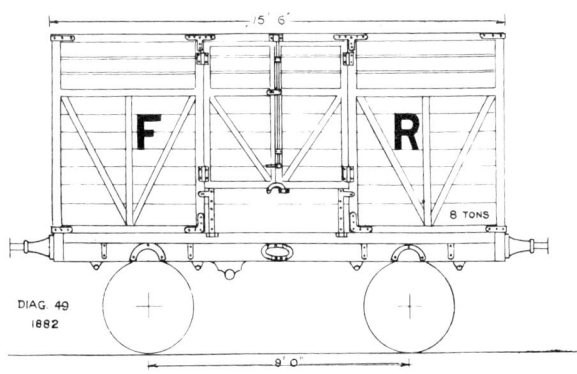
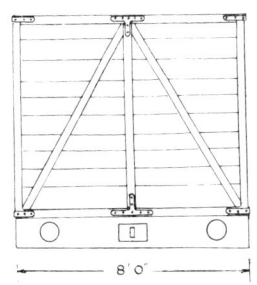

F **R**
8 TONS

DIAG. 49
1882

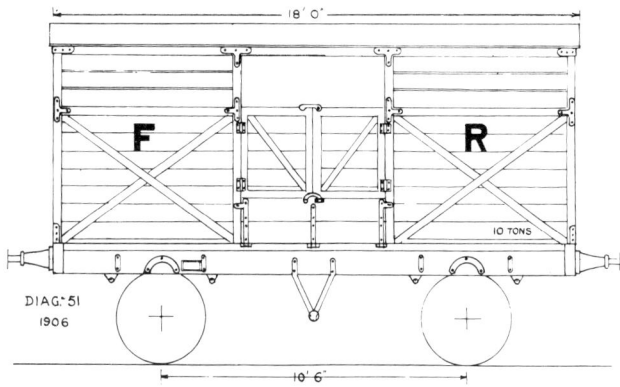

18' 0"

F   R

10 TONS

DIAG.ᵗ 51
1906

10' 6"

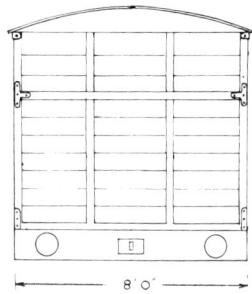

8' 0"

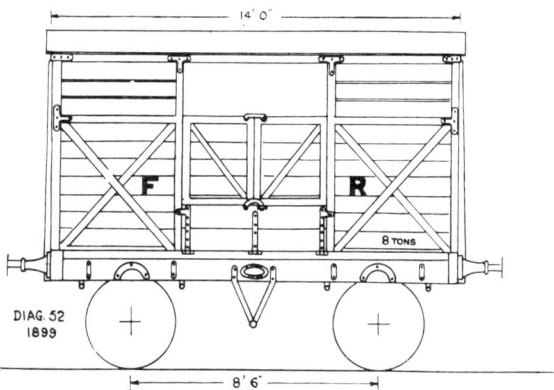

14' 0"

F   R

8 TONS

DIAG. 52
1899

8' 6"

8' 0"

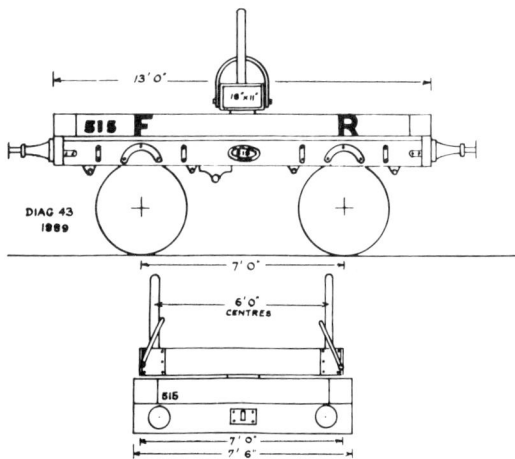

13' 0"

18" x 11"

515 F   R

DIAG 43
1889

7' 0"

6' 0"
CENTRES

515

7' 0"

7' 6"

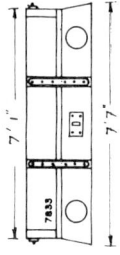

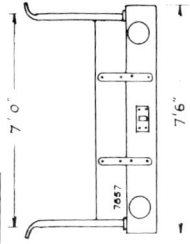

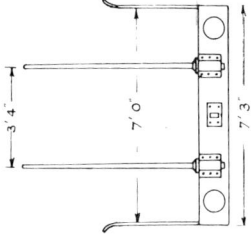

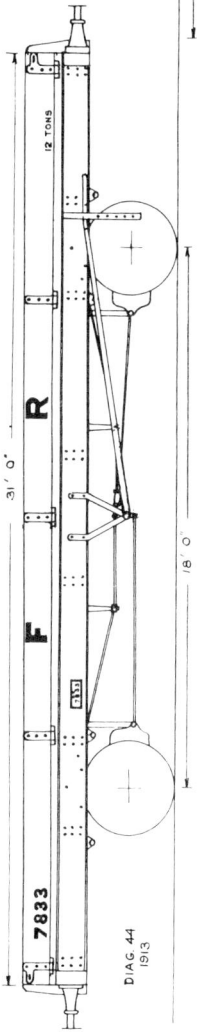

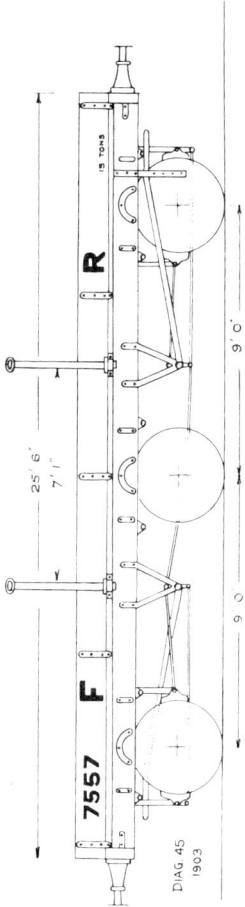

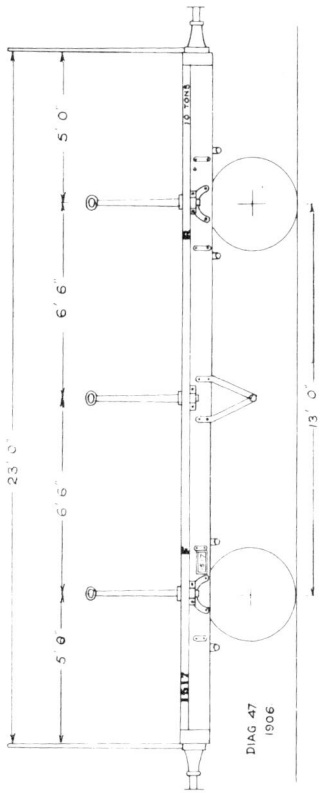

DIAG. 44
1913

DIAG. 45
1903

DIAG. 47
1906

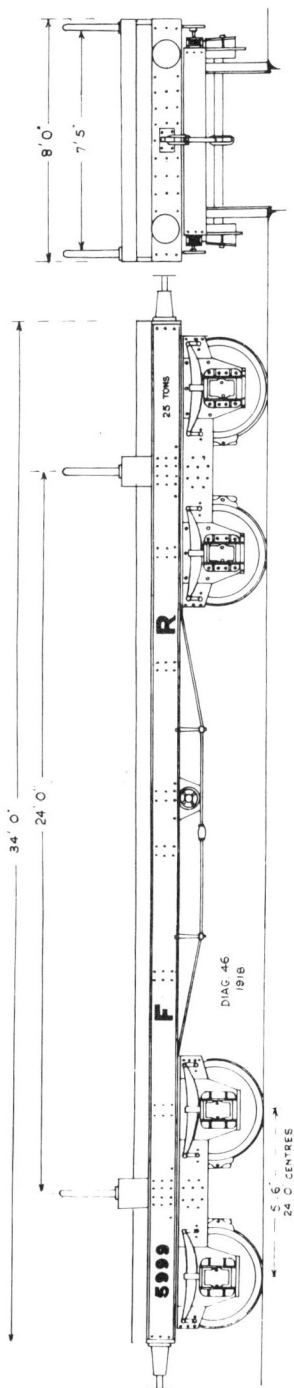

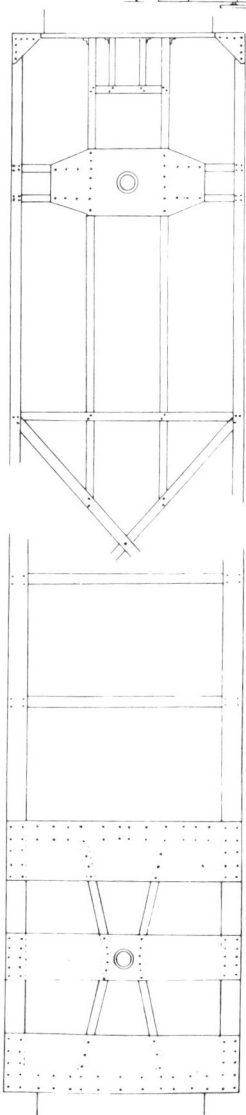

UNDERFRAME PLAN, DIAGRAM 41.

UNDERFRAME PLAN. DIAGRAM 46

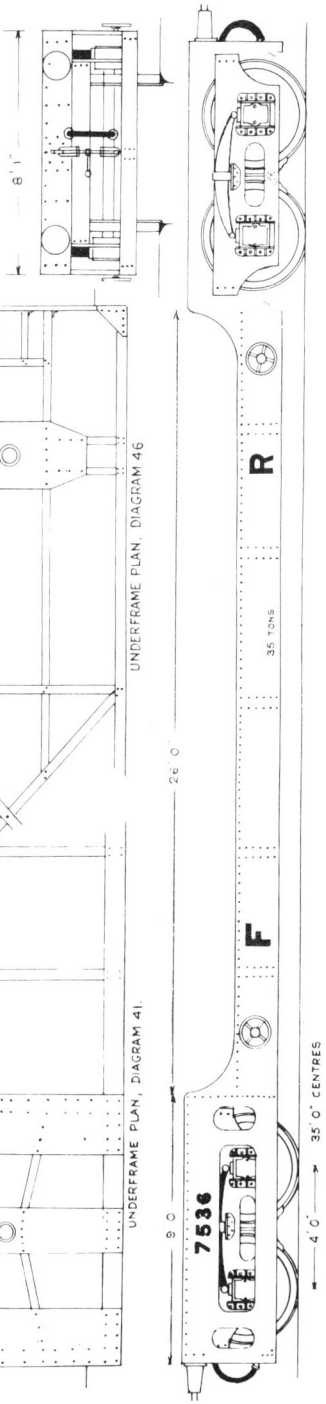

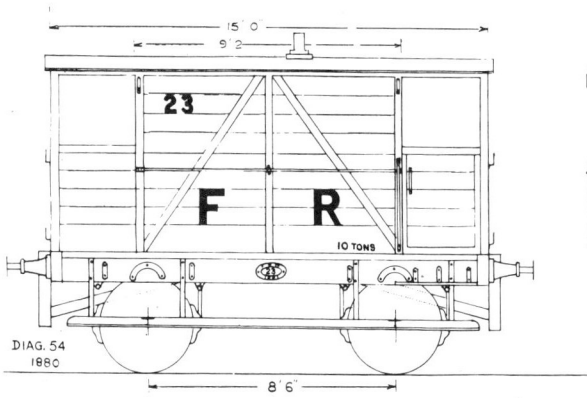

15' 0"
9' 2"
23
F R
10 TONS
DIAG. 54
1880
8' 6"

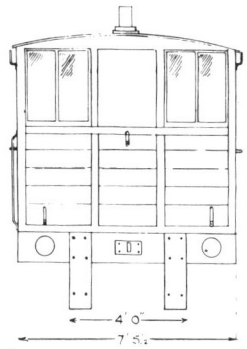

4' 0"
7' 5½"

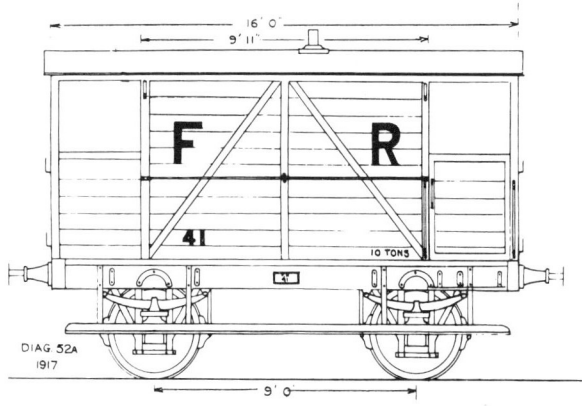

16' 0"
9' 11"
F R
41
10 TONS
DIAG 52A
1917
9' 0"

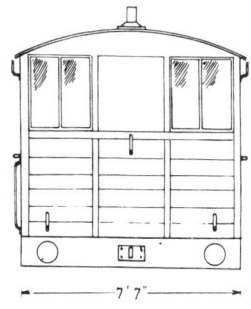

7' 7"

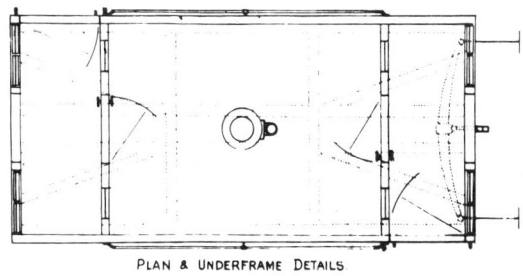

PLAN & UNDERFRAME DETAILS

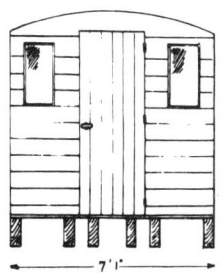

7' 1"